THE CAROLINA PLAYMAKERS

The First Fifty Years

By WALTER SPEARMAN

With the assistance of
SAMUEL SELDEN

The University of North Carolina Press
Chapel Hill

This book is dedicated to Proff Koch and Harry Davis, who helped build The Carolina Playmakers in the past—and to Mary Lindsay Spearman, Jean Herring Spearman, and Emily Crow Selden, who may be considered representative of thousands of dedicated Playmakers through the years, but who also happen to be the collaborators' favorite Playmakers in the present.

Foreword

"An epic struggle of this century," state the authors of *Theater in America* spiritedly, "was the effort of a small group of realistic idealists to create an educational theater. It was not easy to bring this sprawling, suspect, and often misunderstood bastard within American college halls." There existed no precedents that could be referred to in England or Europe; there were no models of standing that could give the theatrical foundling academic sanction. University administrators and faculties "held out against inclusion of the study of theater as long as they could; and when they could hold out no longer, they charily conceded a tiny spot in the curriculum for dramatic literature." Literature, not practice. The century was fairly well advanced before courses in the techniques of the stage—playwriting, acting, directing, scenery and costume designing—began to appear in college catalogues in anything like regular patterns.

When one looks at the handsome theatre buildings that show their faces in increasing numbers on American campuses and meets the crowds of specialists and students who inhabit them today, one finds it hard to realize how bitter was once the struggle against their admission to the realms of education. For more than two hundred years the cultured, as well as the uncultured, man in this country related himself to the concept of practical action. Though maybe he lived in a mansion, wore expensive clothes, and never soiled his hands directly in labor, he did run a plantation, or engage in trade, or spend his working hours in a bank or factory office. In one way or another he regarded himself as a pioneer involved with other pioneers in a concerted effort to conquer a new, untamed continent. Pre-eminently just that.

Art in this period could not be regarded as being a very masculine preoccupation. Portrait and landscape paintings, violin playing, and singing did attract a pleasurable attention in a casual way, but they were regarded as diversions chiefly, more appropriate for the entertainment of the ladies than of their husbands and sons. The men who permitted themselves to be engaged in art as a livelihood were assumed to be those who were not fitted by nature to labor in "more productive fields." This attitude was especially strong toward theatre.

How vigorous was the opposition of the scholarly world toward the stage in early years is indicated in the words attributed to President Timothy Dwight of Yale College in an essay published in 1824: "If the Author has succeeded in proving that the Stage is an evil at all, he has, in proving that it is one of the first magnitude. An evil so great, contagious and extended, ought to get universal opposition in its progress."

Whether these lines were actually written by President Dwight or by someone who appropriated his name we do not now know for sure. We do have evidence to show, however, that they represented a prevailing attitude in the Puritan New England of his day. Twenty-seven years before, in the more liberal South, General William Richardson Davie, one of the leading trustees of the new University of North Carolina, wrote to his friend, James Hogg: "As to acting plays at the University, I think they are by no means as well calculated for improvement in elocution as single speeches, and I believe this will be found to be the result of experience of every college either in Europe or on the continent, in which they have been generally laid aside. . . . If the faculty insist upon this kind of exhibition, the trustees must interfere." General Davie concluded his letter feelingly. "Our object is to make the students men, not players."

Though this attitude was directed specifically toward the stage, the fathers of the University apparently had doubts about the appropriateness of all the arts. We are informed that the North Carolina acts, 27 and 55, promulgated in 1824, protected student morals by insuring that no concert, serenade, or performance in music, singing, or dancing could be given within five miles of Chapel Hill without faculty permission secured at least a week in advance.

Today our Carolina campus boasts a big music building, twice enlarged and crying for more space, and a fine art museum and studio building filled with creative activity that has long since outgrown its present quarters. As late as 1927, when I came to Chapel Hill, there still existed a trace of the old prejudice or at least a lack of enthusiasm about the arts. There was no regular auditorium for musical programs. Chamber concerts were given occasionally in the little Playmakers Theatre (it did exist) and Lamar Stringfield, I recall, had presented his first playing of his Pulitzer Prize-winning *Cripple Creek Suite* on a small stage with the musicians practically sitting in each other's laps. There was no record shop in town. The few available records were dispensed from one end of a counter in Sutton's Drug Store; and the choice was pitifully slim. I remember trying at one time to secure a Straus waltz for a background effect in one of our plays and having to take a bus to Raleigh, thirty miles away, to find it.

The Student Entertainment Committee decided bravely one year to vary its wholly popular offerings with something a little more "cultural." The performer the Committee selected for this unfortunate spot was the eminent violinist, Albert Spalding. Just before the recital a crowd of several hundred irate students protested so vociferously in front of Memorial Hall that the opening of the concert had to be delayed for half an hour until the outside commotion could be quieted. The students were objecting to the way they had been "gypped." To express the force of their indignation they flung their season ticket books into the gutters surrounding the building.

In 1927, there was no art department at all. A painter from Raleigh, who drove over to Chapel Hill to give private instruction to interested individuals once a week, asked if he could exhibit some of his works. When he failed to find any other place on the campus to hang his canvases, Professor Koch generously invited him to stand them up on old chairs in the basement of our theatre. Very few people took the trouble to look at them. After the paintings had been in the basement for about a fortnight we had to remove them because the janitor had entered a complaint to the Buildings Department that the paintings were interfering with his cleaning operations!

In 1927, Professor Koch's The Carolina Playmakers was already nine years old. By this time the playwriting and performing group had extended itself beyond a nucleus of students in the English Department and included men and women from the Law School, Journalism, the French Department, Mathematics, Engineering, and several other areas of the University community. They were working together actively and dedicatedly. Mr. Koch and his young associates had accomplished all this in spite of the fact that, as I have already suggested, they had few precedents they could refer to in the field of playwriting and not many more— at least in the growing years—in play production in other American universities.

That is, there were few precedents except Mr. Koch's own. Before he came to North Carolina he had engaged himself in initiating and building at the University of North Dakota a group of Dakota Playmakers. The group had the same aims—the writing and producing of their own plays—as those that later motivated the Carolina troupe. Koch went to North Dakota in 1905. In 1909, he was at Harvard at the time George Pierce Baker was founding the Harvard Dramatic Club (the famous "47 Workshop" did not appear until 1912), and Koch was doubtless strongly influenced by Baker's beginning work in the teaching of playwriting. In 1911, Thomas Dickinson created the Wisconsin Players which had as one of their primary purposes the production of new plays. In 1912, Thomas Woods Stevens opened a theatre at Carnegie Institute of Technology which developed in the next year into a department of drama. Alexander Drummond organized a dramatic curriculum at Cornell in 1912. All of these activities were far from North Dakota.

Mr. Koch's work at North Dakota was special in that, like Mr.

Baker's, it was oriented toward original writing. It differed from Baker's in its emphasis on "folk" themes. It differed from the productional work of most of the other active pioneers in that the acting and directing grew out of and around the writing. Robert Gard, who has done such outstanding creative work among rural areas through the Wisconsin Idea Theatre, studied with Professor Drummond and fashioned his own program after he left his teacher.

The real flood of university drama departments did not start until the late twenties and early thirties. And it did not begin, of course, as a rush. First, there were limited theatre curricula at such progressive institutions as Iowa, Northwestern, Western Reserve, Mills, Smith, and a few others. Few of them stressed dramatic composition. All of the educational groups of the beginning years were composed of brave individuals who had little to depend on except their own dogged wills and the supporting enthusiasm of a few devoted friends.

Today, more than 800 institutions of higher learning in the United States offer instruction in drama leading to a degree. In nearly 90 per cent of our junior and senior colleges more than 10,000 productions of plays are staged annually in about 1,600 campus playhouses before an audience of approximately 5,000,000 people. The American Educational Theatre Association has a membership of 6,000. Approximately three times this number of people are earning a living in educational theatre.

But to reach this state of activity educational theatre has had to work hard. The present book describes one of the first of the organizations. It has now celebrated its fiftieth anniversary of continuous activity.

The author of this volume is a senior professor of journalism at The University of North Carolina at Chapel Hill. He has been closely associated with The Carolina Playmakers almost from the beginning. In just how many of their plays Walter Spearman has appeared—in Chapel Hill, Raleigh, Charlotte, Asheville, New York, Boston and St. Louis—I cannot tell. I doubt very much if he himself can remember how many!

Samuel Selden

Contents

Illustrations

Illustrations, courtesy of Aycock Brown, Dept Conservation & Development, U.N.C. Photo Lab., and Wootten-Moulton.

THE
CAROLINA
PLAYMAKERS

The First Fifty Years

I. Proff Comes
to Chapel Hill

No star of Bethlehem, or even of Chapel Hill, North Carolina, presided at the birth of The Carolina Playmakers in the fall of 1918. No Wise Man was wise enough to predict that when that irrepressibly enthusiastic Proff Koch came from North Dakota to North Carolina to work with a group of amateur college actors he was launching a theatrical project that would produce a Pulitzer Prize-winning playwright, Paul Green (*In Abraham's Bosom*), a prodigious American novelist, Thomas Wolfe (*Look Homeward, Angel*), and the creators of two widely popular novels, Frances Gray Patton (*Good Morning, Miss Dove*) and Betty Smith (*A Tree Grows in Brooklyn*).

Who would predict that out of The Playmakers would grow a whole series of outdoor dramas that would popularize American history under the stars for millions of American theatre-goers (*The Lost Colony, Unto These Hills, The Stephen Foster Story*)?

Who would predict that in fifty years Carolina Playmakers would write and produce approximately a thousand plays from the fresh and vigorous dramatic materials of their respective communities?

Who would predict that out of The Playmakers would come one
of the most popular television stars, one of the top directors of the
best television drama, successful actors on Broadway and in Hollywood, authors of New York plays and movie scripts, accomplished
actors of stage, screen, and television, authors of dozens of books,
and teachers and play directors at schools and colleges across the
country?

At that particular moment in the history of American drama,
stars were not shining very brightly on the stage. From 1915 to
1919 there was an average of 124 new plays in New York each
year and 72 plays on tour each year. But no Pulitzer Prize for
drama was even awarded in 1918-19. The first Pulitzer had gone to
Jesse Lynch Williams' *Why Marry?* the previous year; and the
1919-20 prize would go to Eugene O'Neill's *Beyond the Horizon*,
a play destined to change the course of American drama; but the
1918 season was bare of distinction.

During World War I and the years following, traveling road companies had declined. College theatres and community theatres
were just beginning to take up the slack and provide what theatrical entertainment was available.

Professor George Pierce Baker had established his famous 47
Workshop at Harvard in 1912. Thomas Wood Stevens established
the Department of Drama at Carnegie Tech in 1913. A. M. Drummond was pioneering at Cornell in 1912.

North Carolina had no great theatrical tradition upon which to
base its new Carolina Playmakers. True, *The Prince of Parthia*, the
first play to be written by an American and produced by professional actors, was written by Thomas Godfrey of Philadelphia at
twenty-two while he was living in Wilmington, North Carolina,
and working as a mercantile agent in 1759.

True, too, North Carolina had its early professional touring
companies in the eighteenth century, presenting plays in Edenton,
Halifax, Wilmington, New Bern, and Fayetteville. Indeed, one
young British actor, Anthony Aston, reports in his brief auto-
biography that in the year 1703, he was washed ashore in North
Carolina after an acting engagement in Charlestown, South Carolina, and was clothed and fed for a month by an "honest North
Carolinian."

In later years, but still long before The Carolina Playmakers
began to tour the state, North Carolina was visited by such
eminent actors as Edwin Booth, Joseph Jefferson, Edwin Forrest,
Otis Skinner, Richard Mansfield, and Mrs. John Drew. It was
almost time for the appearance of The Carolina Playmakers when
Maude Adams visited North Carolina in 1916 in Barrie's *The
Little Minister.*

One early North Carolina playwright, Lemual Sawyer, should
perhaps be mentioned, since his play, *Blackbeard* (1824), was not
only the first play written by a native of the state, the first with
North Carolina characters, and the first with a North Carolina
setting, but it was also an early example of the very kind of native
material the first Playmakers would be using in 1918.

Early Drama at UNC
But of all the early history of North Carolina drama, the incident
most directly affecting The Carolina Playmakers is the story of
William Augustus Richards, a young London adventurer who
deserted his ship in Norfolk, Virginia, and joined a traveling
theatrical company which left Richards stranded in Warrenton,
where he found a job teaching in a local academy. In 1796, he
answered an advertisement of the trustees of The University of
North Carolina and took a job at the preparatory school to the
University in Chapel Hill. With his help, the University's two
literary societies, the Dialectic and the Philanthropic, presented
two plays at the commencement exercises in July, 1796. These
plays are cited as "the first dramatic performances ever given at
any state university in America" and they were performed in Old
East Building, the oldest building on the campus of any state
university.

The plays may indeed have made dramatic history, but they did
not please "the father of the University," William Richardson
Davie, general and Governor, who wrote to his friend James Hogg
in August of 1797: "Our object is to make these students men,
not players." After Richards' death in 1798, Judge Archibald D.
Murphy wrote: "His acquaintance with the stage to some degree
vitiated his morals and gave an air of affectation to his manners.
But these defects he greatly corrected before his death, and

counterbalanced by his many good qualities of mind and heart."

But through the years, University of North Carolina students wanted to be players as well as men.

In 1896, the first play was produced by a regular dramatic organization of students. This was *The Little Rebel*, given by an all-male cast in Gerrard Hall. By 1915, the casts were still all-male and the theatre was still Gerrard Hall, which was obviously not designed for stage productions. There were no dressing rooms; and the actors had to put on their costumes in the Y.M.C.A. building next door and slip into Gerrard Hall through a window. The University Dramatic Club was very active, however, encouraged by its faculty advisors: George McKie and John Booker of the English Department, George Howe of the Latin Department and Archibald Henderson of the Mathematics Department (biographer of George Bernard Shaw).

Mangum Weeks of Alexandria, Virginia, John Y. Jordan, Jr., Raleigh attorney, and Sidney Blackmer of Salisbury (later a distinguished American actor of stage, screen, radio, and television) recall these early days with fond enthusiasm. They remember productions of Pinero's *The Magistrate* in 1913-14, Shaw's *Arms and the Man* in 1914-15, and August Thomas' *The Witching Hour* in the fall of 1915. Lacy Meredith of New Bern and Bruce Webb of Asheville were praised for their skill in portraying the feminine roles, but Elizabeth Lay (now wife of playwright Paul Green) made University theatrical history by becoming the first coed actress when she played the feminine lead in *The Man of the Hour.* Herschel Johnson of Charlotte (later a prominent diplomat) and Charles L. Coggin of Salisbury were other actors of the period.

Dougald MacMillan, recently retired from the UNC English Department, whose early play, *Off Nag's Head,* was produced in 1920 (Jonathan Daniels, now of the *Raleigh News and Observer,* played an old fisherman), recalls that in 1917 Omega Delta, an organization to promote the study of poetry and drama (they met every week and ate apples), held a play contest. First prize of five dollars went to a freshman named "P. Green" (better known later as the Pulitzer Prize-winning playwright, Paul Green) for a play

about the marriage of University President Swain's daughter to a
Yankee. It was produced in the spring of 1917 on the first program in the outdoor Forest Theatre.

Except for this occasional dramatic activity at the University,
there was so little interest in drama shown throughout the state
that Samuel French and Company had crossed North Carolina off
its list of prospective patrons. And, in 1920, H. L. Mencken would
write in his famous essay, "The Sahara of the Bozart":

> If the whole of the late Confederacy were to be engulfed by a tidal wave
> tomorrow, the effect upon the civilized minority of men in the world
> would be but little greater than that of a flood on the Tsang-tse-kiang. . . .
> In all that gargantuan paradise of the fourth-rate there is not a single pic-
> ture gallery worth going into, or a single orchestra capable of playing the
> nine symphonies of Beethoven, or a single opera-house, or a single theatre
> devoted to decent plays, or a single public monument (built since the war)
> that is worth looking at, or a single workshop devoted to the making of
> beautiful things.

This was the time. This was the place. The stage was set—and
soon Professor Frederick Henry Koch would make his entrance
and take over the stage.

Frederick H. Koch (Proff)

Frederick Henry Koch was born September 12, 1877, in Covington, Kentucky, from German stock on his father's side, French
Huguenot, Mississippi-planter on his mother's. As a child he was
fascinated by the theatre and would practice elocution and recite
roles from plays for hours in an upstairs bedroom behind closed
doors. His father was opposed to smoking, drinking, and the
theatre. After graduating from Peoria High School (his family had
returned to their old home in Peoria after staying in Kentucky
long enough for their son to be born a southerner), Frederick attended Caterals Methodist College in Cincinnati, then Ohio
Wesleyan University, where he was graduated in 1900.

In 1905, Koch became an instructor of English at the University
of North Dakota and began his career of teacher, director, and
inspirer of playwriting which was to reach its culmination later at
The University of North Carolina. At North Dakota, Koch pro-

duced Sheridan's *The Rivals* as his first play and took it on tour around the state. Deciding he needed more training, Koch went to Harvard, received his Master's degree in 1909, and returned to North Dakota, bringing with him new ideas on theatre from his favorite Harvard professor, George Pierce Baker. His subsequent productions continued to include the classics but, in 1913, he turned to the Irish dramatists and presented Lady Gregory's *Spreading the News,* Synge's *Riders to the Sea,* and Yeats's *The Hour Glass.* These were plays "of the people," with simple, elemental emotions and poetic colloquial speech, that led, naturally and inevitably, to the original "folk plays" of North Dakota and later of North Carolina.

First came a communal effort of drama students, *A Pageant of the Northwest* (1914) written by a class of eighteen undergraduates from Dakota history and legends. Then on December 19, 1916, came the first series of original one-act plays written by individual students and presented by the newly formed Sock and Buskin Society. One enthusiastic member of this group was Maxwell Anderson, who would later write *What Price Glory* with Laurence Stallings, *Elizabeth the Queen, Winterset* and many other plays, and would win the Pulitzer Prize, as did Paul Green from the North Carolina group.

These one-act plays were toured around North Dakota and met warm reception from the people of the state, who saw their own experiences and history recorded on the stage. Koch wrote of the plays: "Such are the country folk-plays of Dakota—simple plays, sometimes crude, but always near to the good, strong, wind-swept soil. They are plays of the travail and the achievement of a pioneer people."

In 1917, the Sock and Buskin Society changed its name to "The Dakota Playmakers," a title to be rephrased the next year in The Carolina Playmakers.

Another legacy from North Dakota to North Carolina was the idea of an outdoor theatre. In North Dakota it was the Bankside Theatre, which utilized the natural curve of a stream to set off the stage from the audience. In Chapel Hill, it would be the Forest Theatre and in later years it would be a whole series of beautiful and extensive outdoor theatres designed for productions of *The Lost Colony, Unto These Hills, The Common Glory,* and many other historical dramas.

Koch to Carolina

Thirteen years of dramatic achievement at North Dakota had brought Frederick Koch a national reputation. In Chapel Hill, another man of vision, Dr. Edwin Greenlaw, head of the Department of English from 1913 to 1925, realized that North Carolina was full of rich material for writers and that Koch was just the man to encourage the prospective writers. With the support of President Edward Kidder Graham he extended an invitation to Koch to join the faculty: "You will have the greatest opportunity to carry out the work that you have developed," he wrote. "The foundations have been laid; we need now a man who can devote himself to building on them. You will find a warm appreciation of your work and a hearty welcome."

The first building tool Proff Koch (as he was soon to be known by all his students) used was his own enthusiasm: for the theatre and for his students. He was given an office in the old library building (now Hill Music Hall) and soon he was a familiar figure about the Carolina campus—a slight dynamic man, in a belted Norfolk tweed jacket, with a flowing black Windsor tie, pince-nez on a black ribbon around his neck, a briar pipe, and followed by his little dog Dixie.

And where had Koch come to spread his gospel of the people's theatre? He had come to The University of North Carolina, which boasted of being the oldest state university in the country to open its doors to students. Chartered by the North Carolina General Assembly in 1789, the University celebrated the laying of the cornerstone of its first building, Old East, in 1793, and the arrival of its first students in 1795.

Carolina students came from the mountains and from the seacoast, from rural farms and from cities of the Piedmont. Chapel Hill was the seat of learning; and the state looked on it with justifiable pride—and sometimes with suspicion that its learning might be a little too liberal. The brilliant President Edward Kidder

Graham died in the influenza epidemic of 1918 and was succeeded by President Harry W. Chase, famous for his courageous defense of the University against threats of a state anti-evolution bill.

Proff believed in his students; and when he believed in them, they began to believe in themselves.

"It was Koch's greatness," says Jonathan Daniels, one of his first students who later became editor of the *Raleigh News and Observer* and author of a dozen or more books, "that he could give to young hams some feeling that the only difference between them and any Drew or Booth was irrelevant, immaterial and imperceptible."

I am not sure I know what a great teacher is. I think Koch was one. He was no great shakes as a scholar. In the theatre, as in his own life, he was often as corny as North Dakota in August. He was never ashamed to be a ham actor to the end of his days—ashamed? O he positively adored to be. In the theatre and in his classroom, however, he was a beautiful egotist who had the rare gift of bolstering and blessing the pride of young "artists" in themselves. Sometimes his students in acting and writing learned more from each other than from Koch but only because Koch was the kind of man who could transmit enthusiasm and set it stirring all around him.

Playwright Paul Green recalls: "Proff then was in the business of raising flowers, flowers of the imagination. His warm personality helped them to take root. And always the timid, out-reaching tendril-twined student tended to unfold and grow in the sunlight of his favor."

The University had no formal course in drama, so Proff created "English 31-32-33—Dramatic Composition, a practical course in the writing of original plays. Emphasis is placed on the materials of tradition and folklore, and of present-day life."

The course was conducted as a seminar, with teacher and students seated around a long walnut table. Each student would read his play. Then his fellow students would discuss, criticize, make suggestions for improvement—all helping each other in plot, characterization, and dialogue.

The first class had thirteen students—twelve girls and one boy, for this was the time of World War I. That one boy was Thomas Wolfe.

After the first class Wolfe came up to Proff to explain his presence: "Proff," he said, "I don't want you to think that this Ladies Aid Society represents Carolina. We have a lot of he-men seriously interested in writing here, but they are all disguised in army uniform now. I tried to get into one myself but they didn't have one long enough for me." Proff later described Thomas Wolfe as "a lanky six-and-a-half-foot tall mountain lad with burning eyes."

Proff believed that his students could write plays, so they proved it for him. He told them, "Write about what you know." And they did.

"In our way of playwriting we try to cherish the creative spark of the student," said Proff. "We encourage him to examine, with understanding and imagination, the eventful happenings in his own life, the characters in his own neighborhood. Then we guide him toward shaping the materials in an appropriate and interesting pattern for the stage."

Tom Wolfe was evidently listening. In the preface to this first play, *The Return of Buck Gavin,* Wolfe write: "It is the fallacy of the young writer to picture the dramatic as unusual and remote. The dramatic is not unusual. It is happening daily in our lives." He was quoting Mr. Koch almost directly.

While these first students were writing their first plays in the fall of 1918, Proff Koch was getting acquainted with his new home— and liking it. He enjoyed the easy informality of Chapel Hill, the shady streets and sidewalks that might take a sudden turn to save some ancient tree, the prevalence of dogwood and redbud and yellow jessamine. He was an enthusiastic gardener and spent much time working with the roses, azaleas, and other flowers in his yard. He never allowed an engagement at the University to interfere with an appointment with his gardener.

Proff came to know many faculty members who could tell him stories and traditions of North Carolina and who became strong supporters of The Carolina Playmakers: Archibald Henderson, Howard W. Odum, Sturgis Leavitt, Dougald MacMillan, George Coffin Taylor, Arthur Palmer Hudson, John M. Booker, Parker Daggett, and many others, some of whom wrote plays for The Playmakers or acted in the plays.

On December 6, 1918, the *Tar Heel*, student newspaper, carried a brief notice of a meeting to be held December 11, for all those interested in dramatics. And on December 15, 1918, Proff started another tradition in Chapel Hill by giving a public reading of Charles Dickens' "A Christmas Carol."

By January of 1919, Koch was ready to launch his Carolina Playmakers and was preparing for his first public production of plays. He gave an illustrated lecture, "Playmakers of the People," on January 27, and the *Tar Heel* reported:

> The Carolina Playmakers, Professor Koch explained in his lecture last night, will begin with a University Community organization, to be open to all students and members of the community who show ability in any branch of dramatic art—acting, playwriting, scene painting, costuming, and any other form of stage craft.
>
> The prime purpose of the organization will be the production of original plays dealing with North Carolina life and people, and the promotion of such playmaking in North Carolina.

After the lecture, names were taken of any members of the audience interested in working with The Playmakers.

On January 31, an authors' reading of new plays was held in Peabody auditorium, with a good audience that was asked to vote on the best three plays for production.

The three plays selected were *The Return of Buck Gavin* by Thomas Wolfe of Asheville, *When Witches Ride* by Elizabeth Lay of Raleigh (now Mrs. Paul Green), and *What Will Barbara Say?* by Minnie Sparrow of Raleigh.

The Return of Buck Gavin was a short play about a mountain outlaw who returned to see his mother and sister and to put some flowering arbutus on the grave of his friend killed in a battle with revenue officers. *When Witches Ride* utilized the folk superstitions of Northampton County, dramatizing an old legend about a witch named Phoebe Ward and her power to put spells on other people. A toad supposed to be her "familiar spirit" was used in the play. These two plays set the pattern for what would become the typical Carolina Folk Play. The third drama, *What Will Barbara Say?* was a light comedy of college life, which was undoubtedly more recognizable to the local audience but did not have the appeal of the strange and the unfamiliar.

Tryouts were held the first week in February; and those who were not chosen for acting roles were enlisted for costumes, make-up, scenery, or publicity.

When no suitable student actor could be found to play the title role of Buck Gavin in Wolfe's play, Proff told the author: "I guess you'll have to play it yourself, Tom. You may not know it, but you really wrote that part for yourself."

"But I can't act, Proff," Wolfe replied. "I've never acted."

"You're a born actor," said Proff, "and you *are* Buck Gavin."

In later years Koch recalled: "I shall never forget his first performance. With free mountain stride, his dark eyes blazing, he became the hunted outlaw of the Great Smokies. There was something uncanny in his acting of the part—something of the pent-up fury of his highland forebears."

Finding a Theatre

But where could these new plays be produced? Koch found Gerrard Hall completely inadequate. He investigated all the buildings on the campus but found nothing satisfactory. Then he discovered the new public school building, several blocks off the campus, but with a comfortable auditorium and a fairly good platform stage.

The Playmakers extended the apron stage into the auditorium, designed an attractive proscenium arch, a canopy over the stage, and a brown curtain bearing the newly designed mask of The Carolina Playmakers. They constructed homemade footlight troughs, tin-can spotlights and a stationary framework for hanging the scenery. They bought cheap cotton sheeting and sewed the strips together to make the three walls of the log cabin set for *When Witches Ride.*

Scenery was built in various places: the school basement, the Engineering School basement, the attic of Alumni Building. Elizabeth Lay Green recalls taking long walks around Chapel Hill to make sketches of authentic log cabins. "We had noted the mellow tones of age and weather," she says, "we had sketched details of mud daubings, window fastenings, shutters, door latches and the like."

Thomas Wolfe as Buck Gavin in his own play, *The Return of Buck Gavin* (1919).

We took what was at hand—evil-smelling carpenter's glue from the hardware store, unbleached bed sheeting, dry colors from house-painters' bins. Mary Thornton, Josie Pritchard and I were to do the painting but we found the process very different from the watercolor sketching of young ladies' schools. First the stage crew boys had to make us frames on which to stretch the dampened muslin which we had previously sewed together into sheets the size of the log-cabin walls. When these sheets had been stretched and tacked and sloshed with nasty-smelling glue-sizing, the feminine Scene Painting Committee took large house-painters' brushes in their timorous hands and approached the canvases, now propped upright against the studio walls.

Finally it was finished, cut from the frames and hauled onto the school-house stage. Then the stage crew had its problems to solve. The three walls of the cabin were mounted on rollers and hung like window frames on the stage framing and at the corners the canvas had to be tacked to the supports behind. This tacking and hammering, together with the bumping and hoisting of the heavy rollers, prolonged the dragging intermission waits—and also got Proff into bad habits of long curtain speeches aimed to help the audience forget the sound.

The Playmakers had plenty of help for these first plays. The program lists the names of twenty-eight volunteer workers from the University staff and the village community. The playreading committee had included Professors Archibald Henderson, George McKie, John Booker, "Parson" Moss of the Presbyterian Church, and Assistant Librarian Charles Baker.

Hubert Heffner, later to join the Playmaker staff, helped Elizabeth Lay with the scenery. Professor Walter W. Rankin of the Mathematics Department helped with the proscenium arch and the curtain. Professor Parker Daggett of the Department of Electrical Engineering handled the lighting. Cornelia Spencer Love of the library staff was in charge of properties and remembers making a toad for the witch in Elizabeth Lay's play from a lump of plasticine. She also remembers that Tom Wolfe had to drink something in *The Return of Buck Gavin* and admonished her to "be sure it is something good!"

First Plays Presented
On March 14-15, 1919, the first bill of Carolina folk plays was presented in the school auditorium, christened "The Play-House" for

that occasion. The University orchestra played. Dr. Edwin Greenlaw, who had brought Koch to Chapel Hill, gave the opening
remarks, declaring that "it is a red-letter night in the history of this
community and the state, a night which will prove historic."

Thomas Wolfe played the title role in his own play, *The Return
of Buck Gavin*, a drama of early days in Asheville. Later Wolfe explained the genesis of his play: "The incident of the story is derived
from a newspaper clipping describing the capture of a Texas outlaw
in a Chicago tenement house. Certainly a far cry from the mountains of western North Carolina. But when the dramatic possibilities of this incident flashed upon me, I immediately started to work
with a set of mountain characters, the principal being Buck Gavin,
a mountain outlaw."

The cast of Elizabeth Lay's play of Carolina superstitions, *When
Witches Ride*, showed the extent to which The Playmakers were a
genuine community theatre. The "witch" was played by Alga
Leavitt, wife of Professor Sturgis Leavitt of the Spanish Department; and in the cast were George McKie, professor of speech, and
George Denny, a commerce student who later became assistant
director and business manager of The Playmakers. Professor Parker
Daggett wrote original music for *What Will Barbara Say?* a college
comedy.

The playbill for the evening announced "Carolina Folk Plays"
and Koch said that as far as he could determine this was the first
use of the term "folk play" in the American theatre.

Explaining the term, Koch said:

> The term "folk," as we use it, has nothing to do with the folk play of
> medieval times. But rather is it concerned with folk subject matter: with
> the legends, superstitions, customs, environmental differences, and the
> vernacular of the common people. For the most part they are realistic and
> human; sometimes they are imaginative and poetic.
> The chief concern of the folk dramatist is man's conflict with the forces
> of nature and his simple pleasure in being alive. The conflict may not be
> apparent on the surface in the immediate action on the stage. But the ulti-
> mate cause of all dramatic action we classify as "folk," whether it be
> physical or spiritual, may be found in man's desperate struggle for exist-
> ence and in his enjoyment of the world of nature. The term "folk" with us
> applies to that form of drama which is earth-rooted in the life of our
> common humanity.

Koch made another point about these "folk plays" based on the everyday life of the North Carolina students who wrote them so enthusiastically in class: "From the first our particular interest in North Carolina has been the use of native materials and the making of fresh dramatic forms. We have found that if the writer observes the locality with which he is most familiar and interprets it faithfully, it may show him the way to the universal. If he can see the interestingness of the lives of those about him with understanding and imagination, with wonder, why may not he interpret that life in significant images for others—perhaps for all? It has been so in all lasting art."

Early Folk Plays

These fresh, new honest, realistic "folk plays" caught on—with student writers, who went on writing; with local audiences, who turned out to see them; with critics, who found them invigorating and moving. Both characters and settings were genuine and simple; and the plays were very different from the romantic dramas of the period.

Soon this kind of drama would hit New York, too: Paul Green's *In Abraham's Bosom*, which would win a Pulitzer Prize in 1926-27; Lulu Vollmer's *Sun-Up* (1923-24) and Hatcher Hughes' *Hell-Bent for Heaven* (1923-24), also a Pulitzer Prize play (both Miss Vollmer and Mr. Hughes were North Carolina natives and their plays had North Carolina mountain backgrounds); Dorothy and DuBose Heyward's *Porgy*; Jack Kirkland's adaptation of Erskine Caldwell's *Tobacco Road;* and Lynn Riggs's *Green Grow the Lilacs.*

Theatre historian Arthur Hobson Quinn, author of *A History of the American Drama from the Civil War to the Present Day*, saw this relationship when he asked how much influence Koch and his Playmakers had on other playwrights of the early twenties. "It is hardly probable," he said, "that the appearance on the New York stage of this string of southern plays, preeminently from North Carolina, could have been entirely accidental." When he spoke in Chapel Hill for the twenty-fifth anniversary of The Playmakers in 1943, he elaborated: "The best way to estimate the significance of the movement known as the Playmakers Theatre is to try to

The Last of the Lowries (1920), Paul Green's first Playmaker play, with Ernest Nieman, Ruth Penny, and Rachel Freeman.

Negro players from St. Augustine's College in Raleigh."

Mr. Heffner appeared as a bootlegger in his own play, along with George Denny as an old mountain moonshiner and Wilbur Stout as his son. Ernest Nieman played Henry Berry Lowrie, leader of the outlaw gang, in the Paul Green play, with Elizabeth Taylor, a distinguished Playmaker actress of this period, as his aged mother. Miss Taylor also played The Old Woman (supposedly Theodosia Burr) in *Off Nag's Head* with Jonathan Daniels as An Old Fisherman.

Out into the State
Even though these new plays were proving popular on the campus, Koch realized that if The Playmakers were to secure full support in a state university, the plays must be taken out to the people of the state. He already had in mind the necessity for securing better theatre facilities for staging the plays than the public school auditorium.

So on May 7, 1920, The Playmakers took their first trip out of Chapel Hill. They gave a benefit performance in the Municipal Theatre in Greensboro for the District Nurse and Relief Committee. Players were housed in the homes of committee members, which set a tradition to be followed on later and more extensive tours. Plays included *The Last of the Lowries, Dod Gast Ye Both!* and *Off Nag's Head*. Reception of the plays by both audience and reviewers was highly favorable.

George Denny recalled that when *Dod Gast Ye Both!* was performed for commencement on June 15, 1920, a local Negro tried to steal the copper still, lent by the Sheriff of Orange County, from outside the rear door of the school auditorium. The still was saved, he says, "by Hubert Heffner's 100-yard dash across an open field in the moonlight."

The Forest Theatre was used again in the summer of 1920 for a production of *Twelfth Night*, with David Reid Hodgin, Jonathan Daniels, Harding Butt, Hubert Heffner, and Helen Reynolds in the cast.

Another step out into the state came October 19-21, when a historical pageant, *Raleigh, the Shepherd of the Ocean*, was produced in Raleigh. Koch had been commissioned to write this pageant when he had first come to North Carolina. He had acted and would act in many plays, but this was the one great experience in dramatic composition by the man who had inspired and would inspire so many of his students to write plays.

The three-night production, sponsored by the Raleigh Woman's Club and directed by Miss Elizabeth Grimball, was presented at the Raleigh Athletic Park as part of the State Fair and drew a crowd of more than six thousand people. A large chorus drawn from nearby towns was trained by Professor Dingley Brown of Meredith College; and advertisements boasted of "brilliant spectacles" and "500 participants."

Beginning with a Prologue featuring a Chorus of Shepherds dressed in white and saluting the spirit of the heroic Sir Walter, the play had five Episodes and an Epilogue, showing Queen Elizabeth at a garden party, Sir Walter bidding farewell to Governor White as he prepared to sail across the ocean, Sir Walter's vision of the New World, Sir Walter's own voyage in 1617, and his execution in 1618.

Although romantic and sometimes sentimental, *Raleigh, the Shepherd of the Ocean* proved so successful an entertainment that it is reported to have stirred one old showman to remark: "That Koch historical show put the Midway completely on the blink the nights he gave it. Bosco and the wild women hadn't a chance till Mister Pageant packed up and moved away." And it drew a review from the *Christian Science Monitor* that said: "The production of the pageant-drama in Raleigh was an achievement of which the inheritors of the Raleigh tradition may be proud. . . . Professor Koch has struck a high standard for others to maintain."

More significantly, the pageant would later serve as a precedent and model for Paul Green's *The Lost Colony* and numerous other outdoor symphonic dramas based on the history of the region in which they were produced.

The following year a similar dramatic venture was launched in Wilmington, with Koch's advice and encouragement. *A Pageant of the Lower Cape Fear Valley* was written by the Wilmington Sorosis Club and produced on the banks of the Cape Fear River, with Miss Grimball again serving as director.

The first of many statewide Playmaker tours came in May of 1921. Traveling by train, The Playmakers visited six towns, presenting one play from their first bill of one-acts, *When Witches Ride,* and two new plays, *The Miser* by Paul Green and *In Dixon's Kitchen* by Wilbut Stout, a comedy of rural life later to be retitled *On Dixon's Porch* to provide an excuse to use a variety of settings. Visiting Greensboro, Charlotte, Durham, Raleigh, Kinston, New Bern, and Washington (N.C.), they were greeted by good audiences and such enthusiastic newspaper comment as "astonishingly clever" (Greensboro), "Hit is scored by Playmakers" (Charlotte), and "great reception" (New Bern). Acting in the plays on this first tour were Anthony Combs, Katherine Batts, Lloyd Williams, David Reid Hodgin, George McKie, LeGrand Everett, George Denny, Alga Leavitt, Mary Yellott, George Winston, and Thornton Gholson.

The Miser had been produced in Chapel Hill in February, along with another Paul Green play, *The Old Man of Edenton*, but the *Tar Heel* had found *The Miser* "a rather overdrawn, gruesome tragedy of domestic difficulties resulting from conflict of farm and mill" and found *The Vamp*, a college comedy skit by Bill Royall of Goldsboro, "the one bright spot sandwiched between two gruesome horrors."

The *Tar Heel* was edited in 1921 by Green's close friend and fellow Playmaker, Jonathan Daniels—but the *Tar Heel* reviewer still felt perfectly free to say, in discussing Green's *The Old Man of Edenton*, that "the entire cast of perpetrators with the unhappy exception of the author perish in the flames to the great relief of the audience."

The *Tar Heel* also reported in February that The Playmakers had gone on a possum hunt one cold winter night "to get closer to the soil."

A letter from University President Harry Woodburn Chase in March congratulated The Playmakers on their year's work and expressed sympathy with their goal of a new playhouse. A Playmaker Theatre Fund had been established in 1920 and all net profits from the plays were to go in this fund toward a satisfactory building. In order to set up this fund members of The Playmakers' executive board each contributed a dime and a penny; and the bank account was opened with a deposit of $1.01. The ultimate goal was $200,000 for a theatre.

President Chase also urged The Playmakers to present plays at the 1921 commencement, reporting to Koch that the University trustees had voted to move their commencement meeting to the afternoon so they could see the plays at night.

In the fall of 1921, The Carolina Playmakers was officially incorporated on October 24, by Koch, President Chase, University Business Manager Charles T. Woollen, Lucius P. McGehee, Dean of the Law School, Alvin S. Wheeler, George V. Denny, and Elizabeth A. Lay. Officers were Koch as president, Miss Yellott as secretary, and George Denny as business manager.

The distinctive emblem of The Carolina Playmakers, a "CP" monogram mask that now appears on Playmaker pins, programs, and in the theatre, was designed in 1922 by Julius J. Lankes, a noted woodcut artist of Hilton Village, Virginia, who also designed an attractive woodcut, made from apple wood from his own orchard and depicting a Carolina mountaineer, a Carolina pirate, and a Carolina cabin.

Drama in Extension
Still keeping in mind his determination to reach out into the state, Koch had set up a Bureau of Community Drama within the University Extension Division along with the founding of The Playmakers in 1919. Koch himself was listed as director, with Elizabeth Lay as the first secretary.

The Extension Division issued a bulletin announcing that "the Bureau aims to encourage the writing of original plays drawn from traditional and local history and also from present-day life of the people. The Bureau will be glad to give advice and criticism of play manuscripts submitted, and to make suggestions to teachers for the promotion of this work."

Through this bureau, The Playmakers gave help all over North Carolina in the organization and productions of drama groups, and in advising on play selection, direction, scenery construction, make-up, and other areas, in lending plays and sometimes in sending out directors. The rapid growth of this extension activity may be seen in the fact that there were calls for 40 playbooks in 1919-20, for 875 in 1922-23, and for 2,150 in 1924-25.

Elizabeth Taylor, favorite Playmaker actress, served as State Representative for the bureau from 1920 to 1923, Ethel Theodora Rockwell from 1923 to 1927, Sarah Gertrude Knott in 1927-28. Irene Fussler took over the job from 1931 to 1934, at which time John W. Parker became representative and later director. Extension courses in play production were given to train leaders to direct dramatic productions over the state; and an annual institute was held in Chapel Hill for play directors.

The state representative traveled around the state, directing plays, assisting in scenery, costumes, and make-up. No charge was made for her services but the organization requesting them was expected to "pay all travelling expenses and provide entertainment." During Miss Rockwell's first year she managed to assist 292 towns by personal direction or by providing needed material. She actually visited 30 communities to direct plays.

To tie all this new dramatic activity and drama organizations together, the Carolina Dramatic Association was announced by Miss Rockwell in December, 1923, and organized in 1924-25, with W. R. Taylor as its first president and Ethel T. Rockwell as secretary. There were 32 groups enrolled that first year, 52 the next year, and 116 by 1927-28.

Miss Rockwell explained that the new association "will strive to inject into home talent performance something more than merely a laugh or a thrill. It will endeavor to introduce into amateur plays some of the beauty, truth and wisdom inherent in the dramatic literature."

The first Dramatic Institute, sponsored by The Playmakers and the new Carolina Dramatic Association, was held in Chapel Hill April 4-5, 1924, with 72 delegates representing dramatic groups in various parts of the state. A banquet on Friday evening was followed by a bill of Playmaker plays; and on Saturday afternoon the first festival production was presented in the Forest Theatre, when casts of Chapel Hill students directed by Miss Rockwell gave *Six Who Pass While the Lentils Boil* and *Sir David Wears a Crown*.

In the spring of 1925, the first annual dramatic festival was held at Chapel Hill, with the best of the eighteen plays given earlier at centers around the state presented for the final contest. During the first years the groups competed with each other, but later they competed against "standards of excellence" and were given awards for their individual achievements.

The early Carolina folk plays had spread from Chapel Hill out to the boundaries of North Carolina, but Koch believed that these "local" plays would also have a national appeal and he wanted them to reach a wider audience.

Published Plays

In the fall of 1922, the first volume of Carolina Folk Plays was published by Henry Holt and Company and included five plays well tested in productions around the state. These were *When Witches Ride* by Elizabeth Lay, *Peggy* by Harold Williamson, *Dod Gast Ye Both!* by Hubert Heffner, *Off Nag's Head* by Dougald MacMillan, and *The Last of the Lowries* by Paul Green.

"They are wholly native—simple plays of the locality, of common experience and of common interest," Koch wrote in his introduction. "North Carolina is rich in legends and in historical incident; she is rich too in the variety and virility of her present-day life. There is in these plays something of the tang of the Carolina soil. There is something of the isolation of her mountains and their sheltering coves; something of the sun and the wind of the farm lands; of the shadowy thickets of Scuffletown Swamp; something, too, of the loneliness of the lives of the fisherfolk on the shifting banks of Nags Head or Cape Lookout."

For persons not familiar with the North Carolina background of these plays Koch added:

> North Carolina extends more than five hundred miles from the Great Smoky Mountains on the western border to the treacherous shoals of Hatteras. In the backlands of these mountains and among the dunes of the shifting coast line may be found "neighborhoods" where the customs of the first English settlers still prevail, where folk-tales still survive in words and phrase long since obsolete to us, handed down by word of mouth from one generation to another through all the years of their isolation.
>
> And in North Carolina, too, we have the ballads and the lore of an outlived past side by side with the new life of the present day. Here are still

the fine old families of the first Cavaliers and the children of the plantation days of the Old South. In contrast with these is the dreary "one-horse" farm of the poor white tenant and the shiftless negro. In greater contrast, perhaps, is the toil of the thousands of workers at the roaring mills.

Here the home talents are still cherished as a means of genuine enjoyment. The people have not broken their connections with the big family of the country folks. They have retained their birthright of pleasure in simple things. It is not strange that from such a spirit of neighborliness a native drama should spring.

A second series of plays appeared in 1924 and a third series in 1928.

The Playmaker staff also doubled in 1924, when Koch added George V. Denny as business manager of The Playmakers and instructor in play production. Denny had appeared as a student actor in the first play, *When Witches Ride,* and would now organize the first subscription audience, book the first tours, and handle publicity before he left in 1926 for New York, where he later became president of Town Hall and founder and director of Town Hall of the Air. P. L. Elmore, while still a student in 1923, was appointed Playmaker stage manager and later replaced Denny as business manager until he, too, left for New York in 1927.

Looking back on his short but very active association with Proff Koch, Denny remarked, some years later:

> God scatters a wide variety of abilities among men. When a man appears to possess an abundance of talents, his fellows refer to him as a genius. Was Frederick H. Koch a genius? I knew him well and intimately during his first eight years at Chapel Hill, eight exciting and productive years during which he became a national figure and set the pattern of his work that endures in expanded form to this day, but I would not call him a genius. He was much more.
>
> Fred Koch lacked the internal chaos and confusion that is characteristic of the genius. He was a man with a single purpose and a clear vision of how to obtain that purpose. Once he saw that vision—a folk theatre for America—he rested neither day nor night as long as he lived.
>
> Yet he had many of the marks of a genius. He had almost infinite patience with the students who wrote his folk-plays; with the young players who acted in them; with the photographer, Mrs. Bayard Wootten, who made a lasting record of his plays for twenty-five years. I've known him to use an entire day to get pictures of three one-act plays which he would consider satisfactory. He would keep from twenty to fifty people waiting

in costume and make-up through lunch and dinner while he worked with
Mrs. Wootten to get just the right pictures of his plays and players. But it
was these pictures that persuaded Lester Markel of the *New York Times*
to publish the first article about The Carolina Playmakers to appear in this
estimable publication in about 1922. Indeed it was the quality of these
pictures that attracted nationwide attention to "Proff"'s work at the
University of North Carolina.

Proff had other characteristics of genius. He had a high regard for the
importance of his own work. And why not? It *was* important and still is.
Some people called it egocentricity. His own picture frequently appeared
in his capacity as director of the plays he had produced. Was this so bad?
He had pictures made of the Forest Theatre with himself as the sole occupant of the theatre. But the Forest Theatre was *his* dream and *his* creation.
These pictures represented *TRUTH*. Was that bad?

Playmaker Tours

During this period of expansion, the state tours were continuing
and spreading out over the state. In 1921, the second state tour included Henderson, Roanoke Rapids, Scotland Neck, Tarboro,
Goldsboro, Wilmington, Red Springs, and Rockingham. Plays were
The Miser by Paul Green, *Trista* by Elizabeth Lay and the popular
comedy, *In Dixon's Kitchen* by Wilbur Stout.

Koch would accompany his actors and during intermissions between plays would come from behind the curtain, take his pipe out
of his mouth, and chat genially with the audience. His first words
were usually, "Well, folks, we're here and we're glad to be here."
Then he would tell them something about the history of The Playmakers, explain the nature of their folk plays and introduce the
authors. He would also announce that copies of the published folk
plays could be bought in the lobby—or sometimes he had his costumed actors hawk the books up and down the aisles (often to
their great irritation!).

Proff would get so enthusiastic talking to the audience that im-
patient members of the cast or crew would have to jerk his
coattails and whisper that the next play was ready to begin.

During 1920-24, The Playmakers made eight state tours, establishing a reputation not only for the honesty and originality of
their plays but also for their genuine entertainment value. The
annual appearances were looked forward to with such anticipation

that when the Playmaker business manager attempted to cancel an engagement in the little mountain town of Candler, he received a telegram from an Asheville attorney declaring that if the performance was canceled a suit would be brought against The Playmakers.

These tours meant hard work and long hours for cast and stage crew—but they were also a picnic. There was much singing on the bus and, since Proff was a great outdoorsman, there was always a picnic somewhere along the way. The bus would stop in a cleared space along some country road, a campfire would be built, and each cast member was given a big, T-bone steak—to cook it as he could and would. Not infrequently a steak dropped from a sharpened stick into the campfire. When it did, all hands would lend assistance by dragging and pushing to retrieve it from the coals, and it would be eaten anyway—with gusto.

In 1922, Gerald Johnson wrote in the *Greensboro Daily News:*

> Such work as that being done by the Playmakers is a stronger and more direct influence yet toward interesting North Carolinians in themselves and in the life around them. The Playmakers have shown the dramatic interest that exists—for him who can find it—in the life of North Carolina as surely as in the life of Troy, or Camelot, or in any fabled city of the Golden Age. The man whose eyes are opened to the strange things that are going on all around him—to the comedy and tragedy, to the heroism and the absurdity, to the sweetness and the sadness of life in his own village—can hardly sink again into the animal sluggishness that only acts of brutality can stir to excitement and interest.

On one of these tours The Playmakers again had trouble with the copper still now used regularly in *Dod Gast Ye Both!* They were nonplused to discover it had disappeared from the schoolhouse where they had unpacked their properties. When they informed the local sheriff of the theft, he said, "Don't worry. I know where I can pick up another one for you."

And he did. On the recommendation of the sheriff, the property master knocked a hole in the bottom of the still, and nobody bothered to steal it in future tours; but it again disappeared on the department's move from Murphey Hall to Saunders. It left Murphey—but never arrived at Saunders—and the suspicion was that it perhaps had gone back into service!

By January of 1925, The Playmakers felt ready to break out of the boundaries of North Carolina for their tour and visited Columbia and Charleston, South Carolina, Atlanta, Decatur, Macon, and Savannah, Georgia, as well as Badin, Lumberton, and Pinehurst in North Carolina.

Their offerings were three of the most popular Playmaker plays: the old reliable *When Witches Ride; Gaius and Gaius, Jr.,* by Lucy Cobb, a comedy of plantation days; and one of the most moving of all their tragedies, *Fixin's,* a play of tenant farm life by Paul Green and his sister, Erma Green. First produced in Chapel Hill in February, 1924, *Fixin's* had a cast of Frances Gray (later Frances Gray Patton, author of the popular novel, *Good Morning, Miss Dove)* as Lilly Robinson, the farm wife, Charles Pritchett as her tenant farmer husband, and Aubrey Shackell as the landlord.

Of all the early Playmaker plays *Fixin's* perhaps had the strongest emotional appeal to its audiences, this little one-act drama of the farm wife who wanted some "purty fixin's" for her bare home, some flowers to grow, a child to love, and of her husband who cannot see beyond the soil he plows and the land he wants, who lets her geraniums get killed for lack of care and their child die for lack of a doctor. The bleak setting of the play brought home to its viewers the desperate situation of poverty-stricken tenant farmers; and the hopeless lack of understanding between husband and wife gave the play a universal significance. When Lily Robinson goes out the door of that shack and says, "I ain't never coming back—never," Paul Green caught a rare moment of genuine emotion that he never surpassed in his longer plays or his symphonic dramas.

This play was so well received on the southern tour that the *Atlanta Constitution* critic wrote: "Never, it would seem, has any stage given us a more perfect gem than *Fixin's.* It gripped the onlooker until the walls of the theatre melted into mist and we lived in the bare shack the Carolina tenant farmer called his home, and we felt our hearts wrung with the tragedy of the life."

The morning after the Atlanta performance a man came up to Koch and said: "I think I owe it to you to tell you of the effect that little play, *Fixin's,* had on me last night—I come from New

Frances Gray (Patton) as Lilly Robinson, the tenant farm wife, in *Fixin's* (1924) by Erma and Paul Green.

York, and I've been seeing the best shows in the theatre there for thirty years. But that little play last night got me so much that, before I went to bed, I went to the Western Union office and telegraphed some flowers to my wife in New York."

On the less sentimental side, Frances Gray Patton recalls the performance when one of the eggs she was frying on stage for her husband Ed was well past the fresh stage, as she observed as she broke it into the frying pan. What should she do? She cooked it, served it to her husband and said firmly, "Eat it, Ed." And Ed did. Playmakers were ever willing to sacrifice themselves for their art.

When Proff Koch spoke at the Southern Regional Folk Festival at Chapel Hill in 1940, he summed up the first 36 tours of The Playmakers, noting that the group had appeared in 120 different towns and cities, presenting 45 folk plays written and produced originally at Chapel Hill, and had played 322 performances to a total audience of more than 300,000 persons.

In 1923, The Playmakers repeated their first success in the Forest Theatre, *The Taming of the Shrew*, with Koch himself playing a lively Petruchio, Russell Potter (later director of the Institute of Arts and Sciences at Columbia University) as Baptista, and Josephine D. Moore as Katharine.

A Chinese student, Chen-Chin Hsiung, appeared at Chapel Hill to study playwriting—and the familiar Carolina folk plays were extended to include China. Proff's advice was still "Write what you know," so he discouraged his new student from tackling the problems of an American marriage and urged him to utilize the legends of Old China. The result was *The Thrice Promised Bride*, an immensely popular play that was published in Theatre Arts, in an anthology edited by Frank Shay, and in the Golden Book. One of the actors in the Chapel Hill production was Kay Kyser, later to become famous as band leader and radio and film actor.

New Theatre Building

In spite of the remarkable success that Playmaker tours had met, the group still lacked any adequate theatre facilities in Chapel Hill. In 1921, The Playmakers had been promised the University law building when a new law building could be built. In the spring of

1924 came the promise of $25,000 to remodel the building, which had been constructed in 1850 as a library and a ballroom at a cost of $10,363.63.

It was the sixth oldest building on the campus and was named for Benjamin Smith, who had been a governor of North Carolina and had given the University 20,000 acres of land. Smith Hall was designed by A. J. Davis, a New York architect, and built by Captain John Berry. The building is in the Classic Revival style and resembles a Greek temple. The capitals are decorated not with the traditional acanthus leaves but with Carolina wheat and corn. Tradition says they were derived from a design by Thomas Jefferson.

Smith Building had various uses indeed before it finally became The Playmakers Theatre. In 1848, the Di and Phi Literary Societies of the University petitioned the trustees to erect a building to be used as a ballroom and for alumni meetings. The request was granted and the Ballroom came into being in 1850. By 1885, another building had been provided for dancing and the Library took over Smith, with a chemistry laboratory set up in the basement. In 1893, it became the University Bath House, with six white tubs installed for the five hundred students. Hot water was even provided on Saturday nights. The Law School was the next occupant and held it until its conversion to a theatre.

One of the University legends, hard to track down, is that during the Civil War Yankee troops from Michigan had stabled their horses in it. One of Chancellor Robert B. House's favorite remarks to students was that ever since that time "Michigan horses have been noted for their courtesy and intelligence and Carolina students for their horse sense."

A stage, a sloping floor that provided clear sight lines for each of the 335 seats, dressing rooms, and offices were put in, but not enough money was left from the $25,000 appropriation to provide for lights, stage curtain, auditorium seats, or stage equipment. An estimate was made that $13,000 was still needed. Koch went to New York to seek help from his friend, Augustus Thomas, a dramatist who had encouraged the Playmaker work and who now took Koch to see the President of the Carnegie Corporation,

The Playmakers Theatre in Chapel Hill, N.C.

Frederick Kepple, who admitted his interest but made no promises.

But in the spring of 1925, while The Playmakers were on tour in Charlotte, President Chase wired Koch: "Check for $13,000 received from Carnegie Corporation for Playmakers Theatre."

Theatre Dedication
And on November 23, 1925, after seven years of inadequate stage facilities, The Playmakers Theatre was dedicated with the Sixteenth Series of Carolina Folk Plays.

One of the plays had been written especially for the occasion, *Out of the Past* by Frances Gray (Patton), a romance of college youth in 1861 with the setting the portico of the theatre building itself at the last dance held in the ballroom before the outbreak of the war. A Negro slave brought the news, "Sumter is fired!" And the last dance ended in the ballroom until the University was reopened five years later.

Out of the Past was not one of Frances Gray Patton's best plays and she remembers that she did not attend the performance because she was unhappy about the cut version that took away some of the anti-war speeches by a professor character. In the cast were Leon Williams, Robert Harper, Walter Creech, Walter Kelly, George Denny, Margaret Ellis, Helen Leatherwood, and David Britt.

Paul Green's popular *Quare Medicine*, a comedy about a quack doctor and a henpecked husband, was the second play on the bill, acted by Claudius Mintz, E. R. Patterson, Helen Leatherwood, and Charlie Gold.

The third play was *Yon Side o' Sunk Creek* by Martha Boswell, a depressing tragedy, with a cast including B. C. Wilson, D. L. English, Jr., Russell Potter, Ellen Mellick, Ethel Crew, M. W. Breeman, Lucile Heath, and David Reid Hodgin.

The student *Tar Heel* carried a factual story covering the dedication in full detail—and a scathing review of the three plays headed "By the Green Room."

> Monday night, the Playmaker Theatre was dedicated with a program of three native works of art amid due pomp and ceremony. Somehow the reviewer was struck by the resemblance which the whole affair bore to a funeral. The University orchestra opened with slow music; Professor Koch

and President Chase made solemn, complimentary orations; then that piece de resistance of all funerals, the corpse, was brought on in three parts. In this case it was the poor bleeding corpse of Art at Carolina. The trio of amateurish efforts offered Monday night proved that even such a highly touted organization as the Playmakers can do little with practically worthless material. *Out of the Past* was simply dull and lifeless. *Yon Side o' Sunk Creek* was an abortive effort at high tragedy, and *Quare Medicine* was crude slapstick.

After that beginning the review grew really rough.

Fortunately, a few days later a letter from Professor Gerald Johnson to Koch gave another point of view on the program. "It is a great pity," wrote Mr. Johnson, "that the *Tar Heel* had no man available with sufficient intelligence to understand and appreciate the spirit of the performance." Johnson then commented on his own "aesthetic delight" at the plays and their "smoothness, precision and professional finish."

But the real significance of this dedication of the "first state-supported theatre devoted to native drama" did not lie in the rather churlish attack of the student newspaper or in the defense of the theatre by its friends. The significance was caught by both Koch in his introduction and President Chase in his dedicatory address.

"We plan to make our theatre an experimental theatre for the promotion of native drama in North Carolina," said Koch, "a State Theatre in the full sense of the word, a radial center for the development of a real People's Theatre."

And President Chase expressed the attitude of the University Administration toward the new theatre when he said:

We therefore dedicate it tonight in the confidence that it may make possible about our common life a little more of the stuff that dreams are made of; that its existence here shall mean a little less monotony, a little more glamour about our days; that the horizons of imagination shall by its presence here be enlarged so that we shall come more steadily and wholly to see the place of beauty and of its handmaiden, art, in a civilization not too much given to its encouragement. To such purposes this building, the first permanent provision for any of the fine arts at the University, is from this night set apart.

Koch's vision of making Chapel Hill "the center for the development of a real People's Theatre" and Chase's hope that the theatre would mean "a little less monotony, a little more glamour" must have been foremost in the minds of many a staff member and many a student in the years to come. New plays by new play-wrights and new performances by new actors would indeed attempt to "enlarge the horizons of imagination" and to en-courage large audiences "to see the place of beauty and art in civilization."

Only the future could reveal how well The Playmakers met this dual challenge.

II. New Theatre
and Tours to the North

With a new theatre in Chapel Hill in which to try out their new plays, The Playmakers confidently returned to their successful touring. Their second southern tour in February of 1926 took them to Norfolk, Williamsburg, Richmond, Baltimore, and Washington with three plays: *Quare Medicine* by Paul Green, *Fixin's* by Paul and Erma Green, and *Gaius and Gaius, Jr.*, by Lucy Cobb.

The *Baltimore Sun* declared that "their three one-act dramas certainly deserve rank with the best original playwriting by any of our little theatres." The *Washington Post* critic wrote: "The Playmakers showed that their talents in playwriting and acting are equal to the highest professional standards."

The enthusiasm the plays engendered colored a little, perhaps, the critical evaluation of some of the metropolitan viewers. But there was no doubt that the plays were fresh and original and that the performances were bringing forth a strong response from the public.

President Calvin Coolidge was not quite so loquacious when Senator Lee Overman of North Carolina presented his native players at the White House. One version reports that the President

apologized for not seeing the Playmaker show because of a previous engagement and said that he found the volumes of published
folk plays presented to him "very interesting indeed." Another
version is that Senator Overman said: "Mr. President, we just
wanted to show you that the South has its share of beautiful girls"
and that the President replied: "I see, Senator, that you are a keen
observer."

In the spring of 1926, after five years of touring with native
North Carolina folk plays, The Playmakers decided that taking full-
length professional plays out into the state instead of the usual bill
of one-act folk plays might prove a welcome change of pace, so in
the spring of 1926, they toured with Frank Craven's comedy, *The
First Year*, and in the fall of 1927 with Oliver Goldsmith's *She
Stoops to Conquer*.

To their surprise they discovered that they had taught their
audiences in previous years to like the local folk plays and now
they were disappointed to be offered something quite different.
As one newspaper put it:

> *The First Year* is a clever comedy and it went over well with our folks. But
> to the few who have loved the Playmakers for their notable work in writ-
> ing and production of folk plays and native drama, the performance
> Saturday night was a dismal failure. It might have been staged and played
> as well by amateurs from any small college or larger high school in the
> state and, if this is what the Playmakers are coming to, North Carolina
> could well dispense with its maintenance of a state owned theatre and all
> that it stands for at the University.

That was that. Only folk plays in the future.

The Playmakers in New York

And the next future event was the first Playmaker invasion of New
York, where American plays were made or broken, along with the
reputations of actors and playwrights. The plays for this November, 1927, tour included the old reliable *Fixin's*; *In Dixon's
Kitchen* (now on a porch), a hilarious play about a farm boy's
courtship written by Wilbur Stout; *Lighted Candles*, a drama of
the Carolina mountains by Margaret Bland; and *The Scuffletown
Outlaws* by William Norment Cox. Three of the four plays were
given in each town.

Shepperd Strudwick as the father in Wilbur Stout's play, *On Dixon's Porch* (1927).

Acting members of the invading troupe were Katherine Batts and John Harden as the tragedy-haunted tenant-farm couple in *Fixin's,* Josephine Sharkey, Helen Dortch, Hubert Heffner, Shepperd Strudwick (later to make his professional way on Broadway and in the movies), Howard Bailey, Bill Cox, and Lawrence Wallace. The scenery was designed and constructed by Sam Selden, who had just joined the teaching staff as technical expert.

Proff particularly enjoyed riding on top of the bus from time to time, chatting with members of the cast. Bill Cox, author of *The Scuffletown Outlaws,* also liked the top of the bus and usually carried his rifle with him, a rifle which had actually belonged to Henry Berry Lowry, the real "Scuffletown outlaw" portrayed in his play. The two men and the rifle could startle almost any town.

New York was not too hard to crack on this first effort. The Playmakers played before standees at each of three performances in Earl Hall at Columbia University; and the critic for the *New York Herald Tribune* commented: "They are true to the life . . . authentic in every detail. They have a quality of verity and a poignant poetic beauty that can be found only in bonafide folk-drama." And in *Theatre Magazine*: "There was no striving for dramatic effect although drama was there in its truest sense—they were just folks, portraying the traditions, the fears, the frustrations and the joys of other folks whose lives had touched theirs in their Southern homeland."

In Philadelphia, The Playmakers had a capacity audience of 2,700 people in the famous Academy of Music and were compared to the Irish Theatre by the *Public Ledger* critic.

They went North again in the fall of 1928 with two Paul Green comedies, *Quare Medicine* and *The Man Who Died at Twelve O'clock,* and Loretto Carroll Bailey's play about North Carolina mill life, *Job's Kinfolks,* one of the new favorites. In addition to Baltimore, New York, and other cities, they played at the Yale University Theatre in New Haven, Connecticut.

The third northern tour in 1929 not only included two performances at the Guild Theatre in Baltimore and two at the Fine Arts Theatre in New York but went on to Hartford, Connecticut, and Boston, Massachusetts. The program included *The No 'Count Boy*

by Paul Green, *Black Water* by Loretto Carroll Bailey, and
Magnolia's Man by Gertrude Wilson Coffin. An alternative program was offered: a full-length version of Loretto Carroll Bailey's
former one-act play, *Job's Kinfolks,* and this was performed in
Baltimore and New York.

Of *Job's Kinfolks*, the *New York Herald Tribune* said: "Bringing
their scenery, their baggage, themselves and their Southern drawl
in a bus all the way from Chapel Hill, the Playmakers attempt to
project honesty, not greatness. And their attempt is met with success because of honesty and energy instead of histrionic ability."

During the 1928 northern tour, Green's *Quare Medicine* was
broadcast from Station WABC on November 25. Just before the
show Laurence Thompson, a leading member of the cast, was in-
jured in an automobile accident and his part had to be played by
the radio announcer.

And on the 1929 northern tour, The Playmakers drew more attention in Boston than they had anticipated when two of the
actresses, author Loretto Carroll Bailey and Muriel ("Op") Wolfe
walked downtown in their somewhat disreputable stage costumes,
talking in deep southern "po' white" dialect and pretending to be
two country girls from Carolina lost in the big city. Boston's Chief
of Police and Boston's Mayor got in on the act and sympathetic
citizens wanted to raise money to pay the girls' fare back home.

After playing to sophisticated audiences in the North and receiving glowing reviews from Baltimore, New York, and Boston
newspapers, The Playmakers may have been surprised at some of
the things that happened to them back home about this time.

Ministers Shocked
For instance, there was the shocked reaction of North Carolina
ministers to the very funny but forthright Carolina mountain
comedy, *A Shotgun Splicin'*, by Gertrude Wilson Coffin, wife of
the esteemed but irreverent head of the UNC Journalism Department, Oscar Jackson Coffin.

The problem in *A Shotgun Splicin'* is whether a mountaineer
will marry off his sister to an unsavory local politician, who is
father of her unborn child, but the issue is settled in the famous

Loretto Carroll Bailey as Kizzie, the grandmother, in her own play, *Job's Kinfolks* (1928).

Gertrude Wilson Coffin, Charles Lipscomb, and Walter Spearman in Mrs. Coffin's play about the Carolina mountains, *A Shotgun Splicin'* (1928).

last line: "'Druther have a bastard in the family than a damn'
legislator!" In Democratic communities The Playmakers always
made the villain a Republican legislator; in Republican communities he was a Democrat. And the audience loved the line, either
way!

The spring 1928 state tour included *Lighted Candles* by
Margaret Bland, *Job's Kinfolks* by Loretto Carroll Bailey, and *A
Shotgun Splicin'*, which included in its cast Mrs. Coffin herself as
a mountain post-mistress, Charles Lipscomb, Walter Spearman,
Lois Warden, Moore Bryson, and Edwin S. Day. The plays were
drawing good crowds and good reviews—until they hit Charlotte—
and the ministers struck.

The Charlotte ministers were obviously upset. At their first
meeting after the Playmaker performance, the city-county health
officer had reported eight thousand cases of venereal disease in the
city, due, he said, "largely to the motion pictures because ninety
per cent of the pictures shown are about sex."

Then somebody brought up the Playmaker play about an unwed
mother and a shotgun wedding. Protest was made to The University of North Carolina and to "the sovereign people of the state."
The following resolution was passed:

As is well known, under the leadership of Professor Koch the students of
the dramatic section of the English Department of the Univ. of N. C. have,
in the last ten years, made such achievements in play writing, staging and
acting as to gain widespread recognition and distinguished commendation.

On the fifth day of May the Playmakers presented three plays, which,
in our opinion, sustained the reputation of the organization for dramatic
ability. But, while we acknowledge the artistic merit, we also declare that
in our opinion one play, *A Shotgun Splicin'*, seriously violated the pro-
prieties.

Before stating further our complaint against the play, let it be said that
it was clean in the sense that it manifested no tendency or purpose to ex-
cite sex impulses. Nevertheless, we believe that it menaced morals,
especially of the young, in that it could not but wound and tend to destroy
the finer sensibilities, which safeguard pure woman and manhood.

We do not believe that tragic violations of the most sacred processes of
life are fit subjects for comedy.

We do not believe that the effort of an outraged father to force marriage between his daughter and her seducer, presumably to secure

> legitimacy for the child born of the illicit union and some rights for the
> wronged woman is a suitable subject to be presented in a high school audi-
> torium for the consideration of an audience composed, in large measure,
> of school children.
>
> We do not believe a young woman should be trained at the state
> university to play the role of an adulteress and the mother of a bastard
> child, whose stage father is another student, a young man playing the part
> of her seducer.

A citizen from Burnsville in the Carolina mountains wrote a letter to President Chase calling the play "too low and vulgar for
decent people to see and hear" and urging The Playmakers not to
take it to New York or "by all manner of means not to play it
outside of the Bowery, and to carry a sufficient amount of disin-
fectant."

But the Greensboro paper reported "censured play is mild," the
Asheville paper reported that "persons in the audience familiar
with the conditions described in Mrs. Coffin's mountain comedy
were delighted with it and proclaimed its fidelity," and other reviewers called the play "the hit of the evening" and applauded
Mrs. Coffin's "clever lines which kept the audience in a continuous
chuckle." And Koch said, "Sorry the Charlotte ministers feel as
they do, but we have no apologies to make and certainly do not
agree with them. This play will harm no one." It was later published in *Carolina Folk Plays, Third Series* (1928).

Tenth Anniversary
In 1928, Koch looked back on ten years of playmaking and found
them worthy of celebration. During this first decade The Playmakers had produced 59 of their own original folk plays by 42
different authors. Eight of these were by Paul Green, who had
won the Pulitzer Prize in 1927 for his *In Abraham's Bosom.*
Thomas Wolfe, the other most famous of the early Playmakers,
had finished the manuscript of *Look Homeward, Angel*, which
would be published in October, 1929.

The Playmakers had made 21 tours, playing in 63 different
towns in North Carolina and in 27 cities in other states. They had
played to 347 different audiences, numbering more than 150,000

people. Two volumes of Carolina Folk Plays had been published and a third was in the press. Out in the state there were 62 independent drama-producing groups and 47 high school dramatic clubs.

The first issue of a handsome little quarterly, *The Carolina Play-Book*, had appeared in March, 1928, and would continue for sixteen years until Koch's death in 1944, carrying scripts of new plays, articles on the drama by local and national figures, and notes about the work of The Carolina Playmakers and the Carolina Dramatic Association.

In connection with the annual spring Drama Festival of the Carolina Dramatic Association, the first Southern Regional Conference on the Drama was held in Chapel Hill, April 5-7, 1928. Not only were drama directors present from various southern states, but the North had sent such notables down to observe this strange new phenomenon in southern drama as Brooks Atkinson, critic for the *New York Times*; Professor George Pierce Baker of Yale and Professor Alexander Drummond of Cornell; Roland Holt of the New York Drama League; Katherine Emmett of Actors' Equity Association; and Barrett Clark, drama critic. Folk plays presented in honor of the visitors were *Lighted Candles, Mountain Magic, Job's Kinfolks*, and *In Dixon's Kitchen*. Paul Green brought in local Negro singers and old-time fiddlers from the hills.

Critic Atkinson returned to New York enthusiastic about "the glowing colors of the peach trees and the Judas trees and the inexhaustible songs of the cardinals and the mocking-birds," but even more impressed with what he had seen of native drama.

In the *New York Times* for April 15, 1928, he wrote, under the title of "South of Times Square":

> Ever since Professor Frederick H. Koch went to the University of North Carolina ten years ago, he has encouraged his students to write of what they have experienced or observed at first hand, and since North Carolina is luxuriant with folks, legends, dialects and a picturesque history, the response has been tremendous. In fact, what Professor Koch has accomplished, not only at Chapel Hill, but through the state, is nothing short of extraordinary. He has been the animating force in the development of local drama in North Carolina, and he is highly esteemed at home and abroad for his discerning industry and his sapient methods of teaching.

"Paul Green," he added, "may be conservatively described as a genius."

Although Carolina folk plays had made the national reputation of The Playmakers during this first ten-year period, the classical and popular theatre had by no means been neglected. Among the full-length plays that had been given were *The Importance of Being Earnest* by Oscar Wilde, *Seventeen* by Booth Tarkington, *The Torch-Bearers* by George Kelly, *She Stoops to Conquer* by Oliver Goldsmith, *Le Malade Imaginaire* by Moliere, *Le Barbier de Seville* by Beaumarchais, *A Thousand Years Ago* by Percy Mac-Kaye, and *An Enemy of the People* by Ibsen.

In the Forest Theatre, there was usually a Shakespearean play every year *(The Taming of the Shrew, Twelfth Night, Much Ado About Nothing, As You Like It, The Comedy of Errors* and *The Tempest*), but other outdoor plays included *Prunella* by Housman and Barker, *The Rivals* by Sheridan, *The Romancers* by Rostand, and *The Poor Little Rich Girl* by Eleanor Gates.

It was the May, 1928, production of *The Tempest* that brought forth the currently famous "mosquito review" by *Tar Heel* Critic Joseph Mitchell: "Sitting on the ground, with an idiotic moon looking cockeyed through the pines, and with mosquitoes buzzing and biting at dramatic moments, one may be entertained in several ways. . . .Urban T. Holmes (University Professor of Romance Philology) as Caliban rolled over the ground very successfully. . . . Major actors finished their roles creditably, although it was easy to detect the influence of latter-day folk theatre on the Elizabethan drama."

The cast included such leading Playmakers of the period as Shepperd Strudwick, Richard Walser, Lois Warden, Harry Russell, Moore Bryson, Alvin Kerr, Charles Lipscomb, Mary Dirnberger, Bob Cheatham, and Edward D. Wilson. It was a notable show!

Expansion of Staff

The Playmakers had become too big and too busy an organization to be operated by one man alone, even a man of Proff's inexhaustible energy. P. L. Elmore became stage manager in 1923, while still a student, and stayed on for two years after his

Paul and Elizabeth (Lay) Green, both of whom wrote plays for The Playmakers.

graduation in 1925, but left in 1927 for professional theatre work in New York and later for a department store executive position. George Denny left in 1926 and later became president of Town Hall in New York.

Hubert Heffner, a Playmaker undergraduate actor and author of *Dod Gast Ye Both!* joined the staff in 1926 as assistant director and headed the Playmaker work in 1926-27, when Koch was on leave. Heffner left in 1930 to head the dramatic work at Northwestern University and later at Stanford University. His performances as an actor are still recalled, especially the title role in *Rip Van Winkle*, the preacher in *Lighted Candles*, and Old Man Jernigan in *Quare Medicine*. He was also one of the most successful business managers The Playmakers ever had.

Samuel Selden, who would later succeed Koch as head of The Playmakers, came to Chapel Hill in 1927 as technical director. He had first become interested in The Playmakers when he saw a production of Dougald MacMillan's *Off Nag's Head* at the Threshold Playhouse in New York in 1922. Later he met Paul Green while serving as stage manager for Green's play, *In Abraham's Bosom*, in New York. Green had asked to meet the man who was producing such an effective wind sound for his play—and it turned out to be Stage Manager Selden.

Born in China, son of a medical missionary, Selden attended the Shanghai American School and came to America at eighteen to serve for a few months in the Army, then to study at Yale. His later professional experience included the Provincetown Playhouse, the Theatre Guild and the Intimate Opera Company in New York, the road company of O'Neill's *Desire under the Elms*, and various resident and traveling stock companies. At North Carolina, he taught courses in scenery, lighting, acting, and directing and soon brought about notable improvements in the technical aspects of the Playmaker performances. At various times he has studied at the New York School of Fine and Applied Art and at Columbia University and is the author and editor of twelve books on the theatre including *Stage Scenery and Lighting, A Player's Handbook, The Stage in Action, Man in His Theatre,* and *Theatre Double Game.* His first directing assignment was *Ten Nights in a*

Samuel Selden, Hubert Heffner, and Proff Koch, the trio of teachers, actors, and directors who galvanized The Playmakers of the late 1920's.

Barroom, with Howard Mumford Jones, Harry Russell, and Shepperd Strudwick in the cast.

Harry Davis, who would become the third head of the department, came to North Carolina in 1931 after teaching at Mississippi State College for Women and directing the Town Theatre in Columbia, South Carolina. He served as technical director and business manager and taught courses in scene design and stage lighting. His wife, Oramae Davis, took over the job of costuming and built up an extensive wardrobe for subsequent Playmaker plays. She served brilliantly in this capacity until her death in 1942.

The Depression Years

The Depression came to North Carolina and to The Playmakers as it came to the rest of the country. Tours had to be suspended in 1930-31 and 1931-32 because prospective audiences lacked money to buy tickets and The Playmakers could not afford to take the risk of traveling. Tours were resumed, however, in 1933, with *Davy Crockett* by John Philip Milhous, *Four on a Heath* by Foster Fitz-Simons, and *Stumbling in Dreams* by George Brown.

The Bureau of Community Drama in the Extension Division also suffered budget difficulties and had to sacrifice the services of the part-time secretary, but both Koch and his assistant, Mrs. Irene Fussler, continued their extension work without remuneration.

On the positive side, the Depression brought about the establishment of the Federal Theatre Project, which, in turn, pumped new strength into North Carolina drama. Koch was named regional advisor for the Southeast; and three Playmaker alumni served, successively, as state director: Mary Dirnberger, Howard Bailey, and John Walker. While the project in the larger cities was concerned with providing employment for actors, creating new audiences, and encouraging new plays, the North Carolina project had a different goal: "to carry out the ideas planted in this state over the past several years by Frederick Koch, director of the Carolina Playmakers and exponent of native drama. The development of a native drama to be presented by the people of this state is the aim of the WPA Federal Theater project in North Carolina."

And Hallie Flanagan, national director of the project, wrote in her book, *Arena*: "The Federal Theater of North Carolina was a singing theater because it grew up around singing men—Paul Green and Professor Koch."

Community drama centers were set up in ten different Carolina cities and productions given of both standard professional plays and newly written original plays using local material. Classes were also set up in acting, playwriting, costuming, and make-up. Even with the ending of the Federal Theatre Project in 1939, drama activity was carried on in several communities by the Recreation Project of the Works Progress Administration under the direction of Joseph Lee Brown, another former Playmaker.

A by-product of the Federal Theater Project of considerable importance to The Playmakers was the coming to the University on a writers project of Betty Smith, Robert Finch, Herbert Meadows, and Grace Murphy. Betty Smith and Robert Finch wrote numerous plays in collaboration and later Betty Smith wrote the famous novel, *A Tree Grows in Brooklyn*. Herbert Meadows became a successful writer in Hollywood.

In 1931, the fourth volume of folk plays, *Carolina Folk Comedies*, was published by Samuel French and included *Magnolia's Man* by Gertrude Wilson Coffin, *Ever' Snitch* by Irene Fussler, *Agatha* by Jane Toy, *Dogwood Bushes* by Wilbur Stout, *Companion-Mate Maggie* by Helen Dortch, *The Lie* by Wilkeson O'Connell, *Cloey* by Loretto Carroll Bailey, and *The New Moon* by Telfair Peet.

Each play listed the original casts and included were such familiar Playmaker actors of the period as Whit Bissell, who later became a popular movie and television character actor, Elmer Hall, William Faucette, Warren Mobley, Penelope Alexander, Peter Henderson, Elizabeth Farrar, Cyrus Edson, Miriam Sauls, M. L. Radoff, Tom Capel, Graham Dozier, Walter Creech, and Claudius Mintz.

Shaw-Henderson Festival

Even in the Depression The Playmakers were willing and eager to celebrate the appearance of good books on the theatre. Proff Koch

and his associates felt that able historians, critics, and biographers
were as worthy of honor as able playwrights. They were especially
happy to show their pleasure when one of these was a friend,
Archibald Henderson, and the book was as fine as *Bernard Shaw:
Playboy and Prophet*.

In February, 1933, The Playmakers presented Shaw's *You
Never Can Tell*, with Foster Fitz-Simons, Sudie Creech, Aileen
Ewart, Martha Hatton, and William Wang in the cast directed by
Harry Davis, and with Professor Samuel Selden making one of his
rare acting appearances in the role of William the waiter.

The festival included a dinner at the Carolina Inn and an address
by Archibald Henderson in The Playmakers Theatre on "Bernard
Shaw as a World Power." Two surprises of the event were the
playing of a recording made by Shaw himself and a greeting sent
by Albert Einstein.

A 1933 departure from the customary folk play was the produc-
tion of a full-length original, *Sad Words to Gay Music* by Alvin
Kerr, a graduate in the class of 1928 then acting in New York. His
play was a sophisticated comedy set in London's fashionable
Mayfair and had been produced by theatre groups in Milbrook and
Westchester, New York. In the cast were Marion Tatum, Eugenia
Rawls, Carl Thompson, Aileen Ewart, and James McConnaughey.

In the same year (November 2-4, 1933), The Playmakers presented Paul Green's third full-length play, *The House of Connelly*,
which had been first produced in New York in 1931 by the Group
Theatre and which The Playmakers would take on tour in 1940.
In the cast were Christine Maynard as Mrs. Connelly, Charles
Lloyd as William Byrd Connelly, Elmer Oettinger as Uncle Robert,
and Patsy McMullan as Patsy Tate. Professor Phillips Russell appeared as Uncle Reuben and Walter Terry, now dance critic for
Saturday Review, as An Idiot Boy.

In addition to his Pulitzer Prize-winning play, *In Abraham's
Bosom*, Green's *The Field God* had been produced in New York in
1927, *Roll, Sweet Chariot* in 1934, *Johnny Johnson* and *Hymn to
the Rising Sun* in 1936.

In 1934, The Playmakers took three of their most reliable folk
plays to the First National Folk Festival in St. Louis, where they

were welcomed by Gertrude Knott, former state representative of the Bureau of Community Drama in North Carolina and now director of the National Folk Festival. The plays presented were *In Dixon's Kitchen, Job's Kinfolks*, and *Quare Medicine*.

And on December 7-8, 1934, The Playmakers presented another new Paul Green full-length play, *Shroud My Body Down*, with music by Lamar Stringfield and a cast including Robert Nachtmann (now Robert Dale Martin, head of casting for CBS), Alton Williams, Fowler Spencer, Patsy McMullan, and Robert du Four. Incidentally, appearing as "One of the Young People" in this play was Vermont Royster, now editor of the *Wall Street Journal*.

The following year, 1935, saw the production of Paul Green's *The Enchanted Maze*, a strong attack on certain types of college education, with a cast including Bedford Thurman, Charles Lloyd, Frank Durham, Gerd Bernhardt, Paul McKee, William Chichester, Walter Spearman, and Beverly Hamer.

In 1936, The Playmakers took *Quare Medicine* and a new Paul Green play written especially for the occasion, *Texas Calls*, to the Texas Centennial in Dallas.

Part of the cast traveled in the "Honeymoon Special," as Professor John Parker, manager for the tour, had just been married to Proff's secretary, Darice Jackson, in the Koch garden and took the players along on his honeymoon.

John W. Parker's Negro play, *Itchin' Heel*, was produced by the Junior Service League in High Point with an all-Negro cast February 17, 1934. This was said to be the first full-length play of Negro people played by an all-Negro cast.

Highlights of the 1930's in Chapel Hill were the outdoor productions in Kenan Stadium of two Greek dramas by Euripides, *Alcestis* and *Iphigenia in Tauris*; the first production of a full-length original play at the Carolina Dramatic Association's spring festival, *Swastika* by Joe Abrams of the Charlotte Little Theatre; two plays of Negro sharecroppers by Fred Howard, *New Nigger*, a one-act, and *Sharecropper*, a full-length drama; and the production of *Hamlet* in 1935, with Koch playing the title role (one reviewer noted that "Hamlet's inky cloak is touched with crimson").

Hamlet was directed by Samuel Selden, with a cast including

Louise McGuire as the Queen, Patsy McMullan as Ophelia, Harry Davis as the Ghost, Robert Nachtmann as Claudius, William Wang as Laertes, William Olsen as the First Grave Digger, and George McKie as the Priest.

Proff Koch had wanted to play Hamlet ever since his high school days in Illinois, when he saw the role performed by the great Italian actor, Salvini the Younger. He had even given one-man readings of the play at Harvard, at North Dakota, and at Chapel Hill; and it was not too difficult for his staff to persuade him to tackle the role in the Forest Theatre when The Playmakers decided to celebrate the centenary of the birth of Edwin Booth, the great American actor, by producing one of his favorite plays.

"Proff embraced the opportunity with enthusiasm," recalls Director Sam Selden, "but as the time drew near to do the play, he was filled with misgivings concerning his ability to handle his rather terrifying task."

The Koch interpretation of Hamlet was unorthodox in that he tried to show a youthful zest and impish whimsicality beneath the somber melancholy of the tortured Dane. The audience responded with enthusiasm. Professor J. O. Bailey, reviewing the play for the *Tar Heel*, wrote:

> Unusual dash was given to the play by Professor Koch's interpretation of Prince Hamlet. Hamlet's "inky cloak" and "customary suit of solemn black" was lined with crimson, and this fact is, I think, symbolic of both the Playmakers' and Professor Koch's interpretation of the play. Professor Koch acted his most difficult role with sensitivity, with self-scorn and *weltschmerz* in the soliloquies, with his personality pressing Claudius to fear and murder, and yet with a pleasing suggestion of youthful scholar-duellist from Wittenberg in his manner.

Among the playwrights of the early 1930's were several who showed a keen interest in fields of work in which they later became prominent. Vermont Royster wrote *Shadows of Industry*, "a drama of the financial world." Don Shoemaker, later editor of the *Asheville Citizen* and then the *Miami Herald*, wrote *Back Page*, "a newspaper melodrama." Elmer Oettinger, Jr., now on the staff of the Institute of Government at the University, wrote *Design for Justice*, "a social commentary." Walter Terry wrote *When Floosies*

Proff Koch playing the title role in *Hamlet* (1935).

Meet, "a comedy of pseudo-artists." Charles Eaton, now a well-known American poet, wrote *Sea Psalm,* "a tragedy of Carolina sea-folk."

During the same period Wilbur Dorsett wrote several plays of Negro life, including *Goldie* and *Queer New World*; and Ella Mae Daniel wrote *Hunger,* "a tragedy of North Carolina farm folk," and *Yours and Mine,* "a comedy of domestic difficulties."

Additions to the staff at this time included John W. Parker as State Director of the Bureau of Community Drama in 1934 and Business Manager of The Playmakers in 1938 and his wife, Darice, as departmental secretary. Paul Green officially joined the staff in 1936 as literary advisor and Professor of Dramatic Art but still had frequent writing commitments in Hollywood. Howard Bailey, former Playmaker, served for a year as Business Manager and instructor in voice and diction but left to become director of drama at Rollins College in Florida. Phoebe Barr, former dancer with the Denishawn group, was never officially a member of the staff but served actively as visiting lecturer and choreographer, creating the chorus dances for the production of *Alcestis* in Kenan Stadium, as well as other plays.

Outside Assistance

The success of The Playmakers in North Carolina attracted assistance from outside.

The Rockefeller Foundation, in 1933, provided a grant of $7,500 "in recognition of the distinctive work in American drama at the University of North Carolina" and this money was used to pay several assistants to help the staff carry on the work in drama.

In 1936, at the final session of the Carolina Dramatic Association's annual festival, Koch announced the establishment of the Roland Holt Theatre Collection presented to the University by Constance D'Arcy Mackay Holt in memory of her husband, who had been vice-president of Henry Holt and Company, publisher of the first three volumes of Carolina Folk Plays. Mr. and Mrs. Holt had visited Chapel Hill in 1928 for the Southern Regional Conference on the Drama.

In a letter to President Frank P. Graham, Mrs. Holt said: "The

Collection is given to the Carolina Playmakers, rather than to the Museum of the City of New York, because of the long friendship that has existed between Dr. Frederick Koch and the Roland Holts, and also because my husband was the first publisher of the *Carolina Folk Plays*. We always held Dr. Koch and their work in the highest admiration, and our visit to the University was a memorable one."

The Holt Collection, "three trunks full of historically valuable materials," covered fifty years of the American theatre, from 1881 to 1931, and included programs, clippings, photographs and scrapbooks, books, and letter files, which are now housed in The Playmakers Collection in the North Carolina Room of Wilson Library.

Department of Dramatic Art

When Koch came to the University in 1918, the drama courses were a part of the English Department. During the subsequent years of growth it became evident that the dramatic curriculum could be more effectively set up in a department of its own.

In 1936, President Graham gave his approval for the creation of a new Department of Dramatic Art to be headed by Professor Koch. New courses were added. Candidates for the M.A. degree were required to take nine courses, six in the Department of Dramatic Art and three in English or Comparative Drama. The required thesis could be written in the field of drama, theatre history, or theatre arts—or an original full-length play could be submitted instead of the traditional thesis. A dramatic seminar was to be conducted by Professors Koch and Selden of the Dramatic Art Department and Professor George Coffman, head of the English Department, to give the students adequate training in bibliography and research methods.

Professor Robert Sharpe of the English Department served as literary advisor to the drama students; and his famous seminar in Modern Drama was one of their favorite courses, with cookies and hot tea, and arguments which were sometimes hotter than the tea.

The production of Shaw's *Androcles and the Lion*, in May,

1937, in the Forest Theatre, might well be considered an all-star production, judging from the later theatrical accomplishments of members of the cast. Androcles was played by Sam Hirsch, later director of the Biltmore Playhouse at Miami Beach, Florida, and now drama critic for the *Boston Herald-Traveler*. The Lion was Professor Urban Tigner Holmes of the University faculty, who was an inveterate Playmaker from the earliest days and is remembered for his unabashed Caliban in *The Tempest*, when he came on stage with a ragged dried fish held fiercely between his teeth, and for his Grave Digger in *Hamlet*, when he wanted to raise his head out of the grave gnawing on a hambone—but was vetoed.

Quiet Sam Selden, later to be second head of the department, played the Keeper of the Lions, and Harry Davis, third department head, played the Captain. Mary Haynsworth, who later acted in New York, was Lavinia; Robert Nachtmann was Ferrovius; and Paul Nickell, director of many television plays for "Studio One" and "Omnibus," was Lentullus. Howard Richardson, author of the popular folk play, *Dark of the Moon*, was Spintho; and Robert Finch, later husband of Betty Smith and co-author with her of many plays, was Caesar. And Betty Smith herself played a Christian Prisoner.

III. The Outdoor Drama

If the development of the American folk play started The Carolina Playmakers on their road toward a national reputation in the theatre, then it may be said that the outdoor dramas, beginning with Paul Green's *The Lost Colony* in 1937, provided still another type of popular people's theatre. It has been estimated that during the years from 1937 to the present time more than 4,000,000 spectators have attended these productions. In the summer of 1968, *The Lost Colony*, father of all the outdoor dramas, broke all its previous records by playing to 64,500 people in its 54 performances.

How did all this start? And why has it proved so popular?

Professor Koch's idea of the "pageant-drama" or the "historical drama," presenting local history with embellishments of music, dance, and spectacle, may be traced back to *A Pageant of the North-West* in North Dakota in 1914 and *Shakespeare, the Playmaker* in 1916. Professor Koch's *Raleigh, the Shepherd of the Ocean*, produced in Raleigh in October, 1920, foreshadowed Paul Green's *The Lost Colony* in 1937 and the other historical dramas that followed.

Raleigh stimulated preparation of pageant dramas by other people: *A Pageant of the Lower Cape Fear* in Wilmington in 1921, *Children of Old Carolina* written and staged by Miss Ethel

Rockwell of the Bureau of Community Drama at Dunn in 1924, *Visions Old and New* by Pearl Setzer in Gastonia in 1924, and *An Historical Pageant of Orange County* by Playmaker Mary Dirnberger at Hillsborough in 1931. Then in 1936 came *Festival of Youth*, written by seven groups of writers and staged at Cullowhee by Playmaker John W. Parker, and *A Century of Culture*, written by some fifty Carolina playwrights under the direction of Koch and produced by Parker, with a cast of more than five thousand actors, at Duke University Stadium at Durham.

But it was *The Lost Colony* in 1937 that gave impetus to the whole round of outdoor dramas across the nation.

The Lost Colony is a "symphonic drama" celebrating the 350th anniversary of the coming of the first English settlers to this continent in 1587. It was produced on Roanoke Island, off the coast of North Carolina, near the actual site of the first colony, whose members disappeared from the pages of history when they were left on the island with insufficient food, hostile Indians nearby, and a constant threat from Spanish marauders on the sea. The story of Paul Green's drama was that the settlers left the site of their colony with friendly Indians when they were challenged by an enemy ship. Tradition in North Carolina is that they intermarried with the Indians and that some of their descendants make up the present tribe of Croatan Indians in the South-central part of the state. The stirring final scene of the drama shows the settlers, ragged, starved, but still courageous in their determination to maintain their freedom, marching away from their fort singing "O God that madeth earth and sky. . . . We walk this way of death alone."

Paul Green's research into the facts of the original "Lost Colony" convinced him that the colonists were in greater danger from the Spaniards, who wanted to keep the New World for themselves, than from the Indians. Excavations of the original fort showed clearly that its defenses were mounted toward the sea (and the Spanish) rather than toward the land (and the Indians).

This new theatrical form of "symphonic drama" differed from

Robert Armstrong addressing the colonists in Paul Green's *The Lost Colony*,
produced each summer on Roanoke Island, N.C.

An Indian dance in Kermit Hunter's outdoor drama, *Unto These Hills*,
produced each summer at Cherokee, N.C.

the old, familiar "pageants" in that it tells a story and focuses on a central core of leading characters, who exert themselves in conflict in a limited period of time. It is filled with the effects of the pageant—crowds, choral music and dances—but its central story is concentrated and intense.

The phenomenal success of the play sprang from Playwright Green's consummate skill in combining elements of very human characters and story with colorful Indian dances, authentic sixteenth-century English music rendered by choir and organ, spectacles of Queen Elizabeth's court, and wilderness scenes in the New World.

The general pattern of *The Lost Colony* was repeated in most of the outdoor drama which followed it. Relatives of lovable Old Tom, the vagabond of the colony, appear again and again in various comic guises in the later plays of Paul Green.

Although there was, at first, no expectation of extending the run of *The Lost Colony* beyond the 1937 season, the success of the show was so pronounced that plans had to be made to continue it. President Roosevelt was among the early visitors who came to see it, and Brooks Atkinson of the *New York Times* gave it a favorable review. In a later year, Mrs. Eleanor Roosevelt drove up to the theatre in a WPA truck—and stayed to enjoy the performance.

Carolina Playmaker participation in the production was extensive. Not only did Professor Sam Selden direct it for the first twelve years and supervise it for four more, but Proff Koch was advisory director, Wilbur Dorsett technical director, Eugene Langston stage manager, Howard Bailey company manager, John Walker lighting director, Walter Preston master of properties, Oramae Davis costumer, and Fred Howard and Mary Haynsworth choreographers of the dances. The fine group of singers came from the Westminster Choir College at Princeton, New Jersey.

Among The Playmakers who acted in the show were Bedford Thurman, Robert Nachtmann (under the name of Anthony Roberts), Fred Howard, Sam Hirsch, Howard Bailey, Eugene Langston, and Lubin Leggett. Practically the entire staff and crew came from Chapel Hill.

With the success of *The Lost Colony*, other communities around the country became interested in staging similar outdoor dramas of their own. In succeeding years, Paul Green wrote *The Highland Call* for Fayetteville, North Carolina, *The Common Glory* for Williamsburg, Virginia, *Faith of Our Fathers* for Washington, D.C., *The 17th Star* for Columbus, Ohio, *Wilderness Road* for Berea, Kentucky, *The Founders* for Jamestown, Virginia, *The Confederacy* for Virginia Beach, *The Stephen Foster Story* for Bardstown, Kentucky, *Cross and Sword* for St. Augustine, Florida, and *Texas* for Canyon, Texas. Faculty members, students, and alumni of The University of North Carolina had prominent parts in the development of most of these undertakings.

After the precedent was set by Paul Green, other playwrights entered the field. Kermit Hunter, who did his graduate work at The University of North Carolina and is now Dean of the School of the Arts at Southern Methodist University, wrote *Unto These Hills*, one of the most phenomenally successful of the outdoor dramas, for Cherokee, North Carolina, where it was first produced in 1950 under the direction of Playmaker staff member Harry Davis.

Kermit Hunter has written more than twenty outdoor dramas, including *Horn in the West* at Boone, North Carolina (directed by staff member Kai Jurgensen for the first four years), *Honey in the Rock* at Beckley, West Virginia, and the 1968 production *The Liberty Tree* at Columbia, South Carolina. Thomas Patterson, another Playmaker staff member, wrote *Old Four-Eyes*, a play about Theodore Roosevelt, produced in Medora, North Dakota, and *Aracoma Story* for West Virginia. LeGette Blythe, one of Koch's first Playmakers, is author of *The Hornets' Nest* produced at The University of North Carolina at Charlotte in the summer of 1968, with Broadway actor Sidney Blackmer as narrator.

The influence of The Playmakers on the outdoor drama has extended even to Alaska, where former Playmaker Frank Brink is director and author of *The Cry of the Wild Ram* at Kodiak. Playmaker Christian Moe directs *The Lincoln Festival* at New

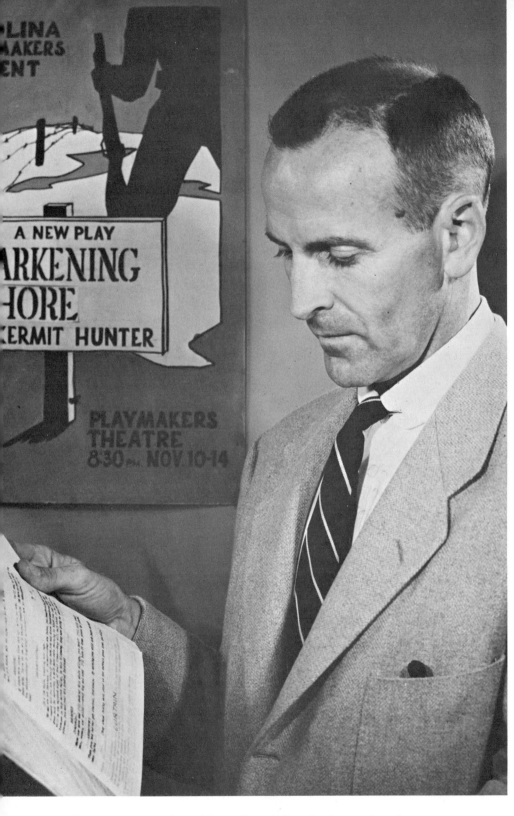

Kermit Hunter, author of *Unto These Hills* and other outdoor dramas.

Salem State Park in Illinois; and Playmaker John Crockett is general manager of *The Legend of Daniel Boone* at Harrodsburg, Kentucky.

These outdoor dramas, most of which are still running, not only draw millions of people to see the shows as a welcome part of their vacation plans, but they also bring a great deal of unexpected money and other prosperity into the communities where the plays are staged, often resulting in permanent improvements in buildings and facilities and raising the local standard of living. The communities around *The Lost Colony* at Manteo and *Unto These Hills* at Cherokee are good examples of these benefits. Houses are painted; stores, restaurants, and motels are erected; children go away to college.

The plays served as excellent training ground for young actors and technicians, many of whom were student Playmakers earning money in summer jobs that increased their experience and proficiency in the theatre. At some of the theatres, special courses in theatre work are set up and canteen shows are given by members of the cast after the regular performances or on free nights, with scenes from Shakespeare, bits of Gilbert and Sullivan, *Hamlet* in modern dress, such full-length plays as *The Night of the Iguana, The Book of Job, Volpone,* and *The Glass Menagerie*, numerous one-act plays, and original cast-written sketches and improvisations. By the use of such devices, student members of the cast gained broader experience than they would have if they limited themselves to acting one role in the outdoor drama all summer.

During the summer of 1966, according to figures issued by the Institute of Outdoor Drama, 24 outdoor dramas sold 1,060,000 tickets. The audience distribution for that year shows some interesting attendance figures: *The Lost Colony* — 58,000; *Unto These Hills* — 120,000; *The Common Glory* — 47,000; *The Stephen Foster Story* — 46,000; *Cross and Sword* — 37,000; *Texas* — 61,000; *Honey in the Rock* — 26,000; *The Legend of Daniel Boone* — 21,000; and *Till the Day Break* (at Winston-Salem) — 20,000.

Betty Smith, author of *A Tree Grows in Brooklyn* and many Playmaker plays, making up for her role in *The Lost Colony*.

Institute of Outdoor Drama

Many of the problems faced by these outdoor dramas were similar and many new producing groups were eager to learn from the experience of earlier dramas, so, in 1963, the Institute of Outdoor Drama was set up in Chapel Hill to provide a clearing house of information and advice.

William Trotman, a Playmaker actor, who had performed brilliantly in his undergraduate days in leading roles in such plays as *Death of a Salesman* and *Under Milk Wood*, became the first director. He was succeeded by Mark Sumner, a Playmaker from his high school days in Asheville, when his original plays had won several prizes at the annual drama festivals, and who later served as chairman of the Department of Dramatic Arts and Speech at Mary Washington College.

The advisory board of the institute now includes such veteran experts in the theatre as Cheryl Crawford, Richard Adler, Mordecai Gorelik, Andy Griffith, Henry Hewes, Christian Moe, Donald Seawell, Betty Smith, and Stanley Young.

New Playwrights Emerging

While the outdoor dramas were being planned, produced, and promoted, a new group of Playmaker playwrights was emerging back in Chapel Hill. The early Paul Green—Thomas Wolfe—Wilbur Stout type of Carolina folk play that had established the beginning reputation of The Playmakers and had been taken on most of their tours was giving way to new plays with cosmopolitan and even international background.

Perhaps Loretto Carroll Bailey was largely responsible for starting this shift with her early successful one-act, *Job's Kinfolks*, which turned to the problems of city and mill people in 1924, and her full-length *Strike Song* (with J. O. Bailey) in 1931, a provocative and exciting play about a controversial North Carolina textile strike. It was reviewed in the *Tar Heel* as "quite the most gloriously ambitious thing ever attempted on their stage" but by the *Southern Textile Bulletin* as "a gross, willful and deliberate misrepresentation of the textile industry." Evidently this forceful play was striking home—and striking sparks.

Josefina Niggli, author of *Mexican Village* and many Playmaker plays set in her native Mexico.

Josefina Niggli came in from Mexico and Gwen Pharis from Canada in the 1930's.

Miss Niggli was born in Monterrey, Mexico, and spent her childhood on an old Mexican estate. The Mexican stories she heard and the people she knew provided authentic background for a series of lively and colorful plays which were first produced by The Playmakers, then taken on various tours, published in a volume, *Mexican Folk Plays*, in 1938, and widely presented in the U.S. and around the world in subsequent years. Her plays included *Tooth or Shave, Soldadero, Azteca, Sunday Costs Five Pesos, The Cry of Dolores, This Is Villa*, and *The Red Velvet Goat*, as well as two full-length plays for The Playmakers, *Singing Valley* and *The Fair-God.*

The plays deal in a vivid and dramatic way—sometimes comically, sometimes tragically—with the childlike, but intensely alive, inhabitants of the small towns of Mexico—carpenters, barbers, soldiers, mayors, housewives, and candy-vendors, supplemented by a few aristocrats and even a French emperor, Maximillian.

Among the actors of this period who brought her plays to life on the stage were Robert Nachtmann, Robert du Four, Ellen Deppe, Christine Maynard, Gerd Bernhart, William Chichester, Hester Barlow, Janie Britt, Mary Haynsworth, John Hardie, and Josephine Oettinger.

Later Miss Niggli wrote a series of connected tales, *Mexican Village*, a portion of which was made into the movie *Sombrero*, and a novel, *Step Down, Elder Brother*. In recent years she has been teaching creative writing and drama at Western Carolina University at Cullowhee.

Gwen Pharis came to Chapel Hill in 1937 from Alberta, Canada, on a Rockefeller Fellowship and wrote four folk plays of her native province: *Still Stands the House, The Courting of Marie Janvrin, One Man's House,* and *Pasque Flower*. Gerd Bernhart, a native of Norway who grew up in South Dakota, wrote *Home-Longing*, with the scene in Norway, and played the leading role herself. Kai Jurgensen, who was born in Copenhagen and reared in Montana, wrote *Tarantula, The Toymaker, Cross on the Door*, and the full-length *Down to the Sea* with the scene in his native country. He later became a member of the Dramatic Art Department staff. Robert Schenkkan, a New Yorker of Dutch extraction, wrote *Black Piet*, a drama of the Boer Commandos. He, too, later taught at the University in Radio-Television-Motion Picture and now heads the radio-television work at the University of Texas. Together, Professors Jurgensen and Schenkkan were responsible for a series of new translations of Ibsen plays.

A second Chinese playwright appeared in this period, Lily T'ang, who wrote a popular Chinese play, *The Wandering Dragon*. It tells the story of an emperor who travels around his country incognito, in search of an unspoiled girl suitable to be his wife, and finds her in an innkeeper's daughter. The search had a doubly happy ending, for the charming young lady who played the innkeeper's daughter later married the young man who acted the part of the emperor.

From Beirut, Lebanon, came Mary-Averett Seelye, who wrote *Fleas and Figs* about her part of the world.

Most of these plays from many countries were published in 1949 in *International Folk Plays*, along with a Negro play, *Washed in de Blood* by Rietta Bailey, and an American Jewish play, *Wherefore Is This Night* by Violet Fidel.

Among the actors in these international folk plays were Robert Carroll, Frank Groseclose, and Sidney Shertzer (all of whom later acted professionally in New York and on television), Josephine Sharkey, one of the Playmakers' most dependable character actresses, Robert Schenkkan, and Jean McKenzie.

The writing team of Betty Smith and Robert Finch (they later became a married team) wrote a series of plays about outlaws, ranchers, cowboys, and mountaineers of Montana: *Western Night, Montana Night, Summer Comes to the Diamond O*. Chase Webb of Silver City, New Mexico, was writing about his part of the U.S. Probably his best play was about the death of Billy the Kid.

But even while the subject matter of Playmaker plays was spreading to other states and other countries, the original idea of Carolina folk plays was never lost.

One of the most talented interpreters of the Carolina scene was Bernice Kelly Harris of Seaboard, North Carolina, who had first been a playwriting student of Koch in the summer of 1919. During the 1930's, Mrs. Harris was writing acutely perceptive and often humorous plays about the people she encountered daily in her eastern North Carolina home community, producing them with a local group of amateur but enthusiastic actors at Seaboard and bringing them to the annual drama festivals at Chapel Hill, where they invariably won top awards.

Seven of these plays were published in 1940 in a volume entitled *Folk Plays of Eastern Carolina* (The University of North Carolina Press). Included were *Three Foolish Virgins, Judgment Comes to Dan'l, Ca'line, Open House, His Jewels, A Pair of Quilts*, and *Special Rates*.

Janie Britt wrote *Leavin's*, a dramatic retelling of an old North Carolina legend about Abraham Lincoln's mother; Frank Durham, *Fire of the Lord*, a play of primitive rural religion and superstition; Lois Latham, *Uncle Smelicue* and *Hello, Hanging Dawg*, Carolina mountain comedies; Fred Koch, Jr., Proff's son who later became head of the Department of Drama at the University of Miami, *These Doggone Elections* and a full-length comedy, *Smoky Mountain Road;* Patsy McMullan, *Cottie Mourns*, a play about Ocracoke Island off the North Carolina coast; Caroline Crum, *Got No Sorrow*, a Negro ritual drama; and Emily Crow (later Mrs. Samuel Selden), *Where the Wind Blows Free* and *Let the Chips Fall*, about her native Texas.

Kate Porter Lewis wrote a series of folk plays about her native Alabama published in the volume, *Alabama Folk Plays*, by The University of North Carolina Press in 1943.

Plays Win Awards

While these plays by a new group of playwrights were first produced in The Playmakers Theatre at Chapel Hill, they were selected for awards in other parts of the country.

Betty Smith's *So Gracious Is the Time* won first prize in the annual Berkeley (California) Playmakers contest for one-act plays in 1938 and her *Three Comments on a Martyr* won the top award the following year. Beverly Hamer's amusing *Funeral Flowers for the Bride*, a favorite tour play, won first place in The International

One-Act Play Competition and was produced at the Duchess Theatre in London in November, 1938. Gwen Pharis' *Still Stands the House* was adjudged the best Canadian play at the annual Dominion Drama Festival at Ottawa in 1939.

Walter Spearman's *Country Sunday*, an anti-lynching play of southern life, won first prize in a contest conducted by the Southern Interracial Commission. William Peery's one-act play, *Thank Rotary*, won first place in an International Rotary contest; and his critical essay on The Carolina Playmakers won first prize in the Leland Stanford University's annual drama contest.

Noel Houston's one-act play about an innocent Oklahoma Negro caught in a white man's court, *According to Law*, was produced by the One-Act Variety Theatre at the Provincetown Theatre in New York in March, 1940.

Junior Playmakers

Back in 1933, Professor Harry Davis had formed a local Chapel Hill group of Junior Carolina Playmakers and produced several children's plays, including *Ali Baba and the Forty Thieves* and *Cinderella*, both of which he had written.

In the summer of 1938, John W. Parker organized the first summer session in Dramatic Art for high school students; and this, too, was called the Junior Carolina Playmakers. Students were given instruction in playwriting, acting, and theatre techniques and received one unit of English credit for their six weeks of intensive work. During that first session thirty-one plays were written and three staged. Professor Parker continued his happy labors with the Junior Playmakers until 1965, when other duties prevented him from dividing his time with the high school group.

Many of the young students who first met The Playmakers in their high school years returned later as college students and again worked with The Playmakers. Among these were Jean McKenzie, William Rawls, James Pritchett, and Tommy Rezzuto.

Theatre Fire

A serious fire broke out in The Playmakers Theatre on August 13, 1938, and caused considerable damage, estimated at $50,000.

John W. Parker, business manager of The Playmakers and executive secretary of the Carolina Dramatic Association.

Investigation indicated that the fire was started by a short circuit in the switchboard on the stage; and fire consumed curtains, scenery, electrical equipment, the stage, and the dressing rooms below.

The exterior of the theatre was only slightly damaged, while the interior was gutted except for the offices at the front of the building. The loss was covered by insurance and the theatre building was restored by January of 1939.

Staff Additions
Earl Wynn came to The Playmakers in 1938 from Northwestern University to become instructor in voice and diction and to organize courses in radio production. Former Playmaker Lynn Gault of Hiram College in Ohio became the first staff designer in 1940.

Under the direction of Professors Wynn and Paul Green classes were held in radio writing and production; and, in 1940, a radio broadcasting studio was set up in Caldwell Hall. Plays were produced every two weeks over a statewide chain of stations and, in March of 1940, a weekly broadcast was started over a nationwide Mutual Broadcasting System network. Some of the earlier Carolina folk plays were adapted for radio by Betty Smith and Robert Finch and original radio plays were written in the classes. Among the authors of these original radio plays were Fred Howard, Sanford Reece, and Weider Sievers.

Also, in 1939, The Playmakers' Film Club was organized for the weekly showing of outstanding films, with discussions conducted by Paul Green. In later years, all radio and film work was transferred to the new Department of Radio, Television, and Motion Pictures under Professor Wynn.

American Folk Plays, a thick volume with twenty plays representing seventeen states, Canada, and Mexico, was published by D. Appleton-Century Company.

Among the plays were such favorites as *Git Up an' Bar the Door* by University Professor of English Arthur Palmer Hudson, *The Last Refuge* by Noel Houston, *Swappin' Fever* by Lealon N. Jones, *His Boon Companions* by Lynn Gault, *West from the Pan-*

Earl Wynn, professor of Radio, Television, and Motion Pictures, in the role of Friar Lawrence in *Romeo and Juliet* (1941).

handle by Clemon White and Betty Smith, and *Day's End* by
Alice Pieratt.

In 1940, The Playmakers made their thirty-seventh tour to ten
cities of North and South Carolina and Virginia, presenting Paul
Green's *The House of Connelly* with Douglas Watson as Will Connelly, Harry Davis as Uncle Bob, Jean McKenzie as Patsy Tate, and
Lillian Prince as Mrs. Connelly.

"Coming of Age"

To celebrate their twenty-first birthday and their "coming of
age," The Playmakers held a regional theatre festival, "Drama in
the South," April 1-6, 1940, with distinguished speakers, native
plays from fifteen southern states and the customary annual
drama festival of the Carolina Dramatic Association.

Guests present for the occasion included Playwrights Elmer
Rice, Clifford Odets, and DuBose Heyward; Brooks Atkinson of
the *New York Times*; George Freedley, Theatre Curator of the
New York Public Library; Arthur Hobson Quinn, theatre histo-
rian; Barrett Clark, secretary of the Dramatists' Guild; Walter
Terry, dance editor for the *New York Herald Tribune*; Norris
Houghton of the Phoenix Theatre; and Robert Porterfield of the
Barter Theatre.

"From the first we have thought of our Playmakers as a fellowship of young people working happily together toward a single
idea—the making of a communal, a people's theatre in America,"
a smiling Proff Koch told his guests and friends at a festival dinner
in the Carolina Inn. "Walt Whitman happily expresses it, 'an institution of the dear love of comrades.'"

Koch also cited a dozen of his former Playmakers for "five-star
awards for distinguished achievement": Jonathan Daniels, George
C. Denny, Jr., Paul Green, Bernice Kelly Harris, Hubert Heffner,
Archibald Henderson, Sarah Gertrude Knott, Kay Kyser, George
McKie, Josefina Niggli, Shepperd Strudwick, and Thomas Wolfe.

Archibald Henderson, who was master of ceremonies for the
dinner, paid tribute to Koch for his twenty-one years of achievement and ended his talk by giving him the new nickname of
"Freddie Folkplay."

Douglas Watson, Harry Davis, and Jean McKenzie (Mrs. Robert Schenkkan) in Paul Green's *The House of Connelly* (1940).

Two features of the festival were the production of Paul Green's play, *The Field God*, with Robert Nachtmann brilliantly acting the lead role, and the revival of The Playmakers' first play, Elizabeth Lay's *When Witches Ride*, with three members of the original cast: George Denny, Jr., Professor George McKie, and Mrs. Alga Leavitt.

Acting in *The Field God* were Robert Nachtmann, Robert Carroll, Roberta Roberson, Patsy McMullan, Sanford Reece, Josephine Sharkey, Eleanor Jones, George Wilson, I. T. Littleton, Mary Wood, Caroline Crum, and Chase Webb.

One session was devoted to a discussion of "Negro Drama in the South" by Zora Neal Hurston and Randolph Edmonds and another to a debate on "Broadway *vs.* the People's Theatre," with George Denny as chairman and Paul Green, Barrett Clark, and Elmer Rice as speakers.

Touring with Redpath

The Playmakers had long dreamed of a repertory company of their own; and, in the fall of 1941, just before the U.S. was plunged into World War II, the opportunity arose. An arrangement was made with the Redpath Bureau for a 16-member Playmaker Repertory Touring Company to take *The House of Connelly* to New York, New England, and the Middle West. The group traveled 8,000 miles to 40 towns and cities in 12 states and played to an estimated audience of 25,000.

Harry Davis was manager of the company and played Uncle Robert Connelly. Other members of the troupe were Robert Carroll as Will Connelly, Barbara Benedict as Mrs. Connelly, Jean McDonald as Patsy Tate, and Carroll Stoker, Mary Wood, Ruth Mengel, Pendleton Harrison, Jane Barrett, David Hooks, Helen Dortch, Jack Rogers, Walter Preston, Eugene Langston, Fred Walsh, and Frances Smith.

The actors had the novel experience of actually being paid Equity salaries—of $40 per week.

The War Years

The first toll of World War II was in taking members of the Play-

Robert Nachtman (Robert Dale Martin) as Mercutio in *Romeo and Juliet* (1941).

maker staff into the armed services—Harry Davis, John Parker, Earl Wynn, Lynn Gault. Temporary replacements on the faculty and in the business office included former Playmaker and versatile actor Douglas Hume, playwright and actress Josefina Niggli, technician Robert Burrows, business manager Joseph Salek, radio instructor Lucile Culbert, and business manager Lynette Warren.

Upon the death of Oramae Davis in 1942, Irene Smart took over the work of the costume department, where she has presided ever since, as well as working with *The Lost Colony* in the summers.

Two new permanent staff members of the department also came to Chapel Hill during this period: Foster Fitz-Simons, former Playmaker actor-playwright and dancer with Ted Shawn and with Miriam Winslow, who came as designer but has also served as director, choreographer, actor, and instructor in dance; and Kai Heiberg-Jurgensen, a native of Denmark, who came to the University as a Rockefeller Assistant and returned in 1944 as director, playwright, actor, and teacher after serving as visiting lecturer at Carnegie Institute of Technology.

The Carolina Dramatic Association sponsored playwriting contests for service men at various training centers in North Carolina; and at the 1943 and 1944 spring drama festivals awards were given to the winning authors. Three of the winning plays were produced in 1944.

Kai Jurgensen served as advisor to the drama group of the German Prisoners of War at Camp Butner, where the crowning achievement was a colorful production by the Nazi soldiers of *Jedermann* by Hugo von Hofmansthal—who was Jewish!

The Playmakers could provide entertainment for the armed services, too—and they did. In 1944, Douglas Hume produced *Boss of Bar Z*, a gala extravaganza, for the Naval cadets at Chapel Hill and, in 1945, he wrote and directed *Playmakers Polyphonic Pastimes*, which was toured to military camps and hospitals in the area.

Playmakers did not forget Proff and The Playmakers when they went to army camps or overseas. They wrote back to Proff and visited him when they were home on leave. He kept up a steady

Kai Jurgensen as Harry Golden in *Only in America* (1962), with Esther
Alexander.

Foster Fitz-Simons and Louise Lamont in *Rain* (1949).

Irene Smart Rains, mistress of the costume shop.

correspondence with many of his boys—and always enclosed a playbill or a program of experimental plays when he wrote.

Perhaps characteristic of the way the soldier-Playmakers felt is this letter from alumnus David Hardison, Jr., still preserved in the pages of the scrapbook:

"Army dress regulation won't let us wear anything that isn't G.I.," Hardison wrote, "but secretly pinned under my left pocket is my Playmakers pin! Sometimes I reach up and touch it or accidentally find it when buttoning up my pockets and then my mind flies through the miles to that brown-columned building in Chapel Hill and it is hard to realize I'm not there, it's hard to 'come back' to Camp Rucker. Proff, I swear that pin is magic! That pin makes me work harder to end this 'business,' it's my own morale builder! It gives me faith and symbolizes what we're fighting for."

Kyser and Feldman Awards

In 1941, Playmaker alumnus Kay Kyser established the Kay Kyser Foundation to provide an annual fellowship covering tuition, room, and board for a student showing special promise of future distinction in the theatre, especially in playwriting. Two future winners of this award would be Edgar Loessin, now head of the Department of Drama at East Carolina University, and Tommy Rezzuto, stage designer for The Playmakers.

Joseph Feldman, considered one of the most promising student playwrights of the late 1930's and early 1940's, was killed in the war in Burma and his father established the Joseph Feldman Playwriting Award in his memory. Feldman's radio play, *In Time, in Space*, had been produced over Station WRAL; and his full-length drama, *Behold the Brethren*, was presented by The Playmakers in March, 1942, after the author had been inducted in the Army. The cast included Lillian Farnol as the Mother, and Robert Carroll, Robert Gutknecht, Arthur Golby, and Frank Groseclose as the four sons. Richard Adler, later a New York composer-author (*Pajama Game* and *Damn Yankees*), reviewed the play enthusiastically as student critic in the *Tar Heel*.

Other original full-length Playmaker plays of this early period of the 1940's included *The Marauders* by Noel Houston, *Remem-*

ber Who You Are by Frank Guess, *Cocky Doodle* by William Maner, *Down to the Sea* by Kai Jurgensen, and *The Twilight Zone* by Tom Avera and Foster Fitz-Simons.

Frank Brink and Barry Farnol were also doing outstanding work in writing and acting both on the stage and in radio. Howard Richardson, who had acted and written for The Playmakers, won the Maxwell Anderson Award in a playwriting contest at Stanford University for his *Barbara Allen*, a full-length play he wrote at Iowa University, with the collaboration of William Berney, which was revised to become the popular *Dark of the Moon*, produced on Broadway in 1945 and by The Playmakers in Chapel Hill in 1954. Interested Playmakers found many resemblances in the play to characters and lines of earlier Playmaker plays.

One of the spectacular productions of the period was Ibsen's *Peer Gynt*, in a new translation by Kai Jurgensen and Robert Schenkkan, produced in the Forest Theatre in May, 1942, with Douglas Watson as Peer, Genie Loaring Clark (later Mrs. Watson) as Solveig, and Jean McKenzie as the Mother. In the cast were such favorite Playmakers as Earl Wynn, Josephine Sharkey, W. P. Covington, III, Tom Avera, Robert Carroll, Elizabeth Trotman, and Anice Garmany.

Douglas Watson was as adept in comedy as in tragedy—and he could sing and dance as well as act. Playmakers who see him now on Broadway or on television still recall his hilarious performance as Bunthorne, "the fleshly poet" in Gilbert and Sullivan's *Patience,* especially the bare big toe that waved thoughtfully in time with the song he sang as he stated his creed as an artist.

Proff Koch appreciated the advantages of good publicity and through these years he had seen to it that The Playmakers secured a good quota of newspaper and magazine space. In collaboration with Bayard Wootten, an extremely talented Chapel Hill photographer, he had made excellent pictures of most of the Playmaker plays. Photographs, clippings, reviews, magazine articles, and programs all were religiously placed in the enormous collection of scrapbooks in the Playmaker office, one volume for each of the productive years.

In the scrapbooks now can be found not only a full record of all current activities of The Playmakers but also a full account of what Playmaker alumni were doing in New York, Hollywood, or elsewhere. These early scrapbooks are full of Paul Green and Thomas Wolfe, but they also have clippings about Shepperd Strudwick playing the leading role in Maxwell Anderson's *Both Your Houses* on Broadway, Eugenia Rawls playing in *The Children's Hour* and with Tallulah Bankhead in *The Little Foxes*, Kay Kyser making a hit in Hollywood, and Whit Bissell appearing in Broadway shows.

The scrapbook takes note of the production of Dougald Mac-Millan's *Off Nag's Head* by the Threshold Players in New York in 1922, of Cheng-Chin Hsiung's *The Thrice-Promised Bride* by the Cherry Lane Playhouse in 1925, and of Paul Green's *In Abraham's Bosom* by the Provincetown Playhouse in 1927 and its subsequent winning of the Pulitzer Prize. There are also accounts of the later productions of Green's *The Field God, Roll, Sweet Chariot,* and *Johnny Johnson*, and of the publication of Thomas Wolfe's *Look Homeward, Angel,* and William Woods's *The Edge of Darkness.*

Articles about The Playmakers appeared in *Theatre Arts Monthly, The Theatre Magazine, The Billboard,* and other magazines—and found their way into the voluminous scrapbooks.

Twenty-Fifth Birthday

The twenty-fifth anniversary of The Carolina Playmakers was celebrated March 25, 1943, in connection with the annual spring drama festival; and a dinner at the Carolina Inn, with Dean Robert B. House presiding, gave the guests an opportunity to wish Proff and The Playmakers a happy birthday.

Barrett Clark was down from New York to speak on "Drama in a Democracy"; and Paul Green, who was away working on a new movie, wrote a letter that was read by Archibald Henderson. Green wrote:

> Twenty-five years I have known you now, and you have held steady and true all that time. . . . May there be twenty-five more fresh and green years for you, young years, years in which you may continue to inspire, to infect with your creative spirit the souls of boys and girls coming on—as you have inspired and touched me.
>
> You have taught us to create our dreams and put them forth into some

sort of human expression—expression on a stage. However crude they may have been at times, you have recognized the realer thing that lies beyond academism, beyond statistics and methodology and beyond finish, the spit and polish of formal appearance. You have always gone back to the springs that bubble with life-giving strength within us. And that is right, has been right and always will be right.

So it is I see you off there, miles apart from me, but moving always with the light—from dawn to noon ascending, from noon to gentle eve gone down. The real and creative life, it seems to me, is like a tree growing, even. And as it builds itself on up it stands at last the first to catch the tip of fire from the rising sun, the last to give up that fire as the night comes on.

Later, at The Playmakers Theatre, three one-act folk plays were presented: *Fleas and Figs* by Mary-Averett Seelye, *The Right and the Left* by Marcelle Clark, and *My World to Grieve* by Walter Carroll, brother of that earlier Playmaker, Loretto Carroll Bailey, and later to be the author of a full-length play, *Tin-Top Alley,* about slum life in Durham, North Carolina.

It was reported that at the twenty-five-year mark, 489 original one-act folk plays had been produced by The Playmakers.

New Forest Theatre
In the spring of 1940, the old Forest Theatre had a face-lifting—
or seat-lifting—job done with $20,000 provided by the Works Progress Administration and improvements designed by Albert Q. Bell, designer of *The Lost Colony* theatre. New stone walls were constructed and tiers of terraced flagstones forming seats were set into the hillside. Two tall stone lighting towers were built. President Frank P. Graham dedicated the theatre May 14, 1943; and The Playmakers presented *A Midsummer Night's Dream*, with the King and Queen played by Foster and Marion Fitz-Simons, the four young lovers by Joan Kosberg, Nell Hill, Russell Rogers, and William Pitts, and the comic players including Robert Burrows, Douglas Hume, Kai Jurgensen, and Peter Strader.

To complete the celebration of the twenty-fifth anniversary, The Playmakers published a commemorative issue of the *Play-Book* in the spring of 1943 dedicated "to the memory of Thomas Wolfe," who had died in 1938. There were tributes to Wolfe by

Koch and Archibald Henderson, letters from Wolfe to his mother and to Proff, and summaries of the Playmaker accomplishments over the twenty-five years. There was a previously unpublished article by Wolfe about The Playmakers and Koch, and quotations from a letter written by Wolfe to Koch in 1933: "I am very proud to call myself one of the Playmakers and to remember that I belonged to the first group you ever taught at Chapel Hill, and had a part in writing and producing some of the first plays. I want to tell you also that no one is prouder than I of the great success the Playmakers have achieved and of the distinguished work which has been done by them."

Death of Proff Koch

The appearance of this commemorative issue of the *Play-Book* with its summary of Playmaker achievements, could not have been better timed. The next summer, on August 16, 1944, while Proff was visiting his son, Fred, Jr., at Miami, he swam out into the sea at Miami Beach, suffered a heart attack, and was drowned, at the age of sixty-seven.

Proff's friends no doubt recalled Paul Green's eloquent letter the year before about the creative life and the growing tree and applied it to Koch himself as "the first to catch the tip of fire from the rising sun, the last to give up that fire as the night comes on."

With Proff's death it was obvious that an era had ended for The Carolina Playmakers—and that a new era would begin. It was also time for a re-evaluation of the 26 years of pioneer playmaking work by this remarkable individual described by Thomas Wolfe as "the man who lived with his idea," by LeGette Blythe as "the merry little man in the Norfolk jacket," and by Paul Green as "the first to catch the tip of fire from the rising sun." Theatre Historian Arthur Hobson Quinn said at the twenty-fifth birthday celebration: "The best way to estimate the significance of the movement known as the Playmakers Theatre is to try to imagine what American playwriting would have been for the last twenty-five years without them."

Certainly Koch was open to criticism—and people gave it to

Proff Koch talking to the cast of *Romeo and Juliet* (1941) in the Forest Theatre. Robert Carroll played Romeo, Robin Bolce played Juliet; and the cast included Earl Wynn, Josephine Sharkey, Robert Nachtman (Robert Dale Martin), and Frank Groseclose.

him. He was too tall a tree in the forest not to attract occasional lightning. And he was too obsessed with his one idea of creating a folk theatre not to let other things slide.

Cornelia Spencer Love, writing for Samuel Selden's *Frederick Henry Koch: Pioneer Playmaker* (1954), noted that in listening to the reading of the new plays in his early Chapel Hill days, "his critical faculties were somewhat in abeyance—all his geese were swans." But Proff's great contribution, she added, "was his insistence that these youngsters, fresh from their schoolrooms, search out the folklore, the history, the everyday living of their native towns and hamlets."

Professor Archibald Henderson, one of Koch's closest friends, described him as "another benevolent monomaniac" like Johnny Appleseed—and nicknamed him "Freddy Folkplay."

Novelist William Woods (formerly Playmaker William Wang) wrote to Proff on that twenty-fifth birthday:

> Speaking quite frankly, Proff, you know as well as I do that they've been criticizing you for many years. They say you publicize yourself. They say you play favorites. They say that every time you make a curtain speech you repeat the same old thing. I don't know how often I have heard you reminisce about Tom Wolfe or the old High School stage, or this or that tour.
>
> But, by heaven, that's the secret. Thank God those accusations are true. For, by whatever method it is, you made each one of us who ever sat in your classes an integral part of the whole quarter century of Playmaker history. You stuffed us so full with Carolina, with bits of your own self, with your sentimentality, your quirks and creeds, your perversity, your faith and your lust for life and for your brand of theatre that long afterwards, when everything else is forgotten, you alone are left.

These early Playmakers knew Proff well and understood him. "Yes, Proff had many of the earmarks of genius," wrote George Denny, Jr., "but I prefer to think of him as a personality inspired by a great dream that carried him through life arousing the creative impulse in others. He was a great teacher because he possessed this ability in such large measure. He was an important influence in the lives of those who did not stay in the theatre because he unleashed their creative talents and inspired them to be themselves with integrity and courage."

Even in the midst of an overwhelmingly good press and genuine acclaim for the early work of The Playmakers, there were certain negative notes that pinpointed weaknesses in the Playmaker approach to drama. Norris Houghton, in his generally perceptive survey of American theatre outside New York in 1941, *Advance from Broadway*, recognized Koch's "matchless enthusiasm" which "has resulted in widespread awareness of theatre throughout the area in which he has worked" and described him as "the arch prophet of regional drama in this country: a drama devoted to portrayal of the warp and woof of simple human experiences in whatever humble environment they occur."

But Mr. Houghton believed that Koch's insistence that "anyone can write a play" and its corollary, "everyone should write a play," had resulted in "a plethora of exceedingly bad stuff—vast fields of weeds." He suspected that "the soft-scented breezes of Chapel Hill and the aroma of Koch's placid pipe combined to work a critical lethargy for which there are but two antidotes."

One of these antidotes was the presence in Chapel Hill of Paul Green: "Among all the artists of the theatre with whom I talked throughout the country," wrote Mr. Houghton, "none had greater vision or wisdom than Paul Green. His playwriting is the epitome of all that Koch seeks in the theatre."

His other antidote was "Mr. Koch's personal enthusiasm which is pervasive and indomitable" but which is "combined with a joyous disregard for any kind of standard—a situation which I regard as too serious to be overlooked."

Mr. Houghton cited criticisms of The Playmakers which had come from inside the family circle, an essay by graduate student playwright William Peery entitled "Carolina Playmaking: A Portrait on Its Coming of Age," which won the 1939 Gray Essay Award of the Dramatists' Alliance at Stanford University.

Mr. Peery, while celebrating the twenty-first anniversary of The Playmakers, warned of "four major flaws in the critical theory of folk playwrights":

> 1. An attempt to preserve the past—not as history but as a living anachronism—may be in practice an attempt to block progress, to deny contemporary life. Carolina folk drama has been too largely an escapist drama.

2. The native drama as practiced by Lady Gregory and the Carolina Playmakers has encouraged "writing down" to the natives. Paul Green was one of the folk . . . but the Playmaker author of the second generation is condescending. . . . Playmaker authors do not necessarily say but frequently imply, "Now isn't that quaint?"

3. Like other arts, drama is at its best a happy marriage of form with content. This delicate balance between manner and matter the writer of folk plays can hardly be expected to attain. Subscribing to a creed which emphasizes content, the Playmaker author either "created fresh dramatic forms" as Professor Koch says or perhaps was careless of form altogether.

4. In their emphasis on the local, in sacrificing form for content, writers of folk plays have not properly evaluated the new content. . . . As a final consequence of emphasizing native content, authors of the folk play have committed the sin unpardonable in the theatre, the crime of being monotonous. . . . The Playmakers have now contributed their tragedy of tenant farm life, their rural comedy, their mountain drama, their epic of the Negro. Should anyone ever try to write a second *Huckleberry Finn*?

Mr. Peery's final warning was that the Playmaker staff "must teach their students to find the dramatic value of native materials where it is and has always been, not in the folk trappings but in the human problems."

This warning came in 1939. How accurate was William Peery's appraisal—and how seriously did The Playmakers take his advice in the years to come?

Certainly one of Koch's great contributions is the firm establishment of a people's theatre—which he called "folk theatre"—as an honest, authentic element in the American theatre, effectively presented to a widening public through the work of his offspring, The Carolina Playmakers. But his other significant contribution, and one that should never be minimized, is his role as a man of affirmation with an abiding faith in his students and in his own creative power to bring out their highest potential. His constant insistence that "of course you can do it" may have produced some poor plays but it also produced talented Playmakers with confidence in their own abilities.

If ever a man witnessed his own immortality—and enjoyed it— that man was Proff!

IV. Samuel Selden, Chairman, 1944-1959

So, in the fall of 1944, Proff was no longer on the campus, with his Norfolk jacket, his pipe, his disreputable tweed hat, his dog Patsy (successor to the deceased Dixie)—and his infectious smile. One of his favorite quotations in recent years had been Walt Whitman's "Expecting the main things from those who come after"—although it was difficult to believe that Proff could possibly expect "main things" to come after.

What did come after was Samuel Selden, who had joined the Playmaker staff in 1927 and had been Koch's No. 2 man. "Quiet and unassuming," Harry Davis wrote of him, "he had been largely responsible for the high professional standards maintained in Playmakers productions, and for the firming up of the academic courses in dramatic art."

Koch had never been deeply interested in the academic aspect of the University. He was more creative than scholarly, more inspirational than pedagogical.

Paul Green recalls:

His way of teaching was not popular with the scientific and scholarly professors. It couldn't be, no matter how much they liked him as a man.

They considered his methods hit or miss. In fact he had no methods. His dislike for painstaking research or historical process offended their outlook and area of values. He was an enthusiast. And findings and contentions of enthusiasts are always in the final analysis—their phrase—likely to be unreliable. They found his class assembly more like a group picnic than a meeting of serious workers.

The transition from Koch Playmakers to Selden Playmakers was not as sharp as one might have expected. In Proff's later years his early dynamic drive had somewhat slackened. He left more and more of the routine but time-consuming business of operating the Department of Dramatic Art to his staff members. They had proved their dedication and their abilities through the years; and even though they must often have felt that they were not receiving due recognition for their services, they kept right on working.

Proff encouraged their expression of imagination and their initiative if he was sometimes reticent about giving them public credit for their work. Privately, he was very appreciative of their help. As for the graduate curriculum, Proff was never very enthusiastic about it. He preferred the old one-act plays, written with fresh excitement by young students out of their own experience, to the longer, more difficult, more demanding full-length plays written in lieu of a thesis. Nor did Proff care for the discipline of administration or the frustrations of University committees. He preferred the free, unfettered soul of the young playwright expressing himself. He longed for the old days of bus rides around the state as The Playmakers took their heartfelt plays to the people.

Selden of course wanted to sustain the reputation of The Playmakers as the leading exponent of the American folk play, but he also wanted to give his department a seriously needed academic respectability, to raise the academic standard of the courses, and to steer The Playmakers into the mainstream of the American academic community.

On his desk one morning he found a letter from "the Dean": "There seems to be a growing disposition on the part of students in the Department of Drama to spend a disproportionate part of their time in stage activities to the detriment of their studies in other fields. We hope that this situation can be adjusted at once. . . .

This letter is not meant to be a criticism of your program, but I do wish to call attention to the fact that our theory has always been that we should not develop in the direction of the conservatory type of education."

This was a situation Selden wanted to remedy—and set about doing so. He believed that a department of drama should offer both general education for students who would not necessarily continue their careers in the theatre and specialized education for those who would enter the field of the professional theatre. There should be "skill" courses, but these courses should also have sound "content." And there should be graduate work, especially for those planning to teach drama. He set forth his philosophy of education in an article for the 1944 *Carolina Play-Book* entitled "Dramatic Art in a University Program."

Having come from the professional theatre in New York to the academic environment of Chapel Hill, Sam Selden knew that he was facing a dilemma in the department he had inherited and the horns of a dilemma are seldom comfortable. Here was the problem: Should the Department of Dramatic Art train its students in professional technical proficiency so they could hold jobs in the commercial theatre—and indeed improve the quality of acting, writing, directing, and designing in that theatre? Or should the department stress the academic side of the theatre and train students to become scholars, teachers, and critics? Or could the department somehow manage to do both?

Long hours of rehearsals and shopwork for students in drama were needed to give them professional competence—but there was little time left to secure a "liberal education" in other areas. Or if they took a regular load of college liberal arts courses, how would they ever become "professional" in their chosen field?

This conflict between professionalism and scholarship was an old one; and it would continue to be a problem for years to come.

Selden attempted to solve this problem—and his dilemma—with what he described as "the double pyramid." This double pyramid would have a single broad base (undergraduate work leading to a B.A. degree) and a double apex (graduate work leading either to a Ph.D. in scholarship or an M.F.A. in creative professionalism).

All students should be graduated with a good, basic grasp of both scholarship and creatorship, said Selden. And here he liked to quote William James's observation that the strength of any society is best judged by the creativeness it induces in its citizens. The evidence of this creativeness exists in their works of art.

After the broad liberal arts experience of his undergraduate program, the drama student could proceed to the M.A. program. The purpose of this program would be to initiate him into the discipline of graduate study, to allow him to try out his talents in one particular theatre field, to extend his background in theatre history and literature, and to give him time and opportunity to consider continuing to a Ph.D. or an M.F.A.

If he continued toward the Ph.D., his program of study would be centered principally on historical, literary, critical, or technical research. If he continued toward the M.F.A., he would follow an intensive course of advanced training in one specialty leading toward a career in the professional theatre or the direction of a university theatre or the teaching of acting, scenic or costume designing, playwriting, or business management.

"No man or woman can expect in the brief time he spends in an academic institution to make himself outstanding in both scholarship and creatorship," Selden pointed out.

The validity of Selden's arguments, as well as the continued conflict between the practical craftsmen and the research scholars, could be noted in a 1962 article, "The University and the Creative Arts," in the *Educational Theatre Journal* by W. McNeil Lowry, director of the Ford Foundation Program in the Humanities and the Arts.

Lowry said: "The university has largely taken over the functions of professional training in the arts but in the main has sacrificed professional standards in doing so." He suggested the necessity of "a radical shift in the university atmosphere surrounding students considered potential artists" and "the provision of postgraduate opportunities for professional apprenticeship removed from an academic environment."

Professors would have to be selected "not so much for their ability to conform to regular academic patterns as for their ability to be stimulating, flexible and imaginative, in a way best fitted to push forward the necessarily somewhat erratic work of their students."

Whereas Proff Koch's emphasis had been on impulsive creativity, Sam Selden wanted to move in two directions: solid academic structure and increased professional proficiency. He wanted to build both apexes of that "double pyramid" of his. But at this point in the history of The Playmakers, the department was not able to set up a Ph.D. program, since members of the teaching staff had been selected for their theatre proficiency and their creative abilities rather than for academic training and Ph.D. degrees. Certainly the Department of Dramatic Art did become a more integral part of the University academic structure. And certainly the Playmaker productions were beautifully designed, handsomely costumed, admirably mounted.

The question must be raised, however, as to whether some of the initial enthusiasm and freshness of The Playmakers were not lost in the shift of emphasis. The experimental one-act plays written by students were still being produced and still elicited lively discussions by the audience, but few were being published or produced elsewhere. The full-length public productions tended to be rather stock classics or old Broadway successes, with few exciting excursions into new areas of theatre.

Postwar Students
Students coming to the University after World War II were more sophisticated and less parochial. Among them were Army veterans who had been in Europe and had seen the excellent professional theatre work in England and France. They were apt to be critical of amateur "school stuff."

The novelty of the Carolina folk play had begun to wane and more drama students were coming from other states. Knowing the reputation of The Playmakers, they felt they had to write about subjects they knew little about—tenant farmers, Negroes, fisherfolk, mountain people. The plays were imitative. Selden felt these students should be encouraged to use their own material and not distort it to fit the old Carolina folk play patterns.

Selden made himself join such national organizations as the
National Theatre Conference, the American Educational Theatre
Association, and the American National Theatre and Academy and
attended their meetings to discover what other theatre leaders
were doing in the nation. He became a committee man and officer
in all of these bodies.

Temporary staff members and lecturers were invited to come to
Chapel Hill to give students some concept of the theatre world at
large. Lennox Robinson, director of the Abbey Theatre in Ireland,
spent the 1946-47 year in Chapel Hill as visiting lecturer and di-
rected the Playmaker production of his own play, *Drama at Innish*.
Hans Rothe, German refugee playwright and translator, was on the
staff in 1947-48, and his play, *Innocence*, was produced in May,
1948. Walter Prichard Eaton, New York critic and old friend of
The Playmakers, was a visiting professor of playwriting in 1949-50.
Cid Ricketts Sumner was on the campus for the production of
Hear the Hammers Ringing, a dramatization of her novel, *Quality*.
And Agnar Mykle of Copenhagen, Denmark, was present for the
production of his *Morning in Yellow-Orange*.

And while Carolina playwrights were still using Carolina material
(*Salt Sands* by Virginia Page Spencer of Swan Quarter, *Snow
Falling* by John Ehle of Asheville, and *Big Meetin' Time* by Clare
J. Marley of Cary), students from other areas were utilizing their
own native background (*Wherefore Is This Night* by Violet Fidel
of Brooklyn, *Subway Rhapsody* by Sam Hirsch of Trenton, New
Jersey, and *Five Notes in a Bar* by Phyllis Jean Sullivan, of New
Bedford, Massachusetts, with George Grizzard, later a Broadway
star, in the cast).

The 100th bill of Playmaker experimentals was presented
December 12, 1944, with *The Distances to Go* by Anne Osterhout
(later Mrs. Harry Davis), *Poor Mr. Burton* by Mary Brooks
Popkins, and *Wings in the Sun* by Mary Lou MacGowan.

Student Playwright Hirsch, whose imaginative works received
mixed student reviews, is now drama critic for the *Boston Herald-
Traveler*. Arnold Schulman, who played a playwright in Hirsch's
Subway Rhapsody, is now a playwright in real life; he wrote
A Hole in the Head first as a play, then as a movie script for Frank

Sinatra, and, in 1968, wrote screenplays for Neil Simon's *Star Spangled Girl* and Philip Roth's *Goodbye, Columbus* (starring Richard Benjamin and directed by ex-Playmaker Larry Peerce).

The Year 1948

The year 1948 might be considered a typical year of Selden's new regime. The Playmakers started off with a rousing production of Gilbert and Sullivan's *The Mikado*, directed by Lynn Gault with music conducted by Paul Young. The rather prestigious cast included Sam Hirsch as Poo-Bah, Andy Griffith as Ko-Ko, the Lord High Executioner, Barbara Edwards (later Mrs. Griffith) as Yum-Yum, Catherine Covington as Katisha, and Sam Greene, who later made his way into the New York theatre. Barbara Edwards moved on to the role of Eleanor Dare in *The Lost Colony* and Andy Griffith to the role of Sir Walter Raleigh, then to Broadway in *No Time for Sergeants*, and to Hollywood films and his own television show.

Drama students, eager as usual to get more theatre experience than the regular Playmaker program could give them, had organized a Student Laboratory Theatre in 1946, which produced *Fashion* in February and a full-length original, *Mr. Luck* by Mildred Howard, in May. In 1949, they did *Gorboduc* in the lounge of the Student Union.

Robert Armstrong, a football player from Bessemer, Alabama, who had won a Frederick H. Koch Scholarship in Playwriting in 1947, converted his 1945 one-act play, *Egypt Lan'*, into a full-length play. This was presented in November, 1948, with Andy Griffith in the tragic Negro role of Mose Rivers and Barbara Edwards as Mamie Lou Johnson. After playing John Borden in *The Lost Colony* for several summers, Armstrong moved on to New York and the part of Big Daddy in *Cat on a Hot Tin Roof* and to other stage, movie, and television roles.

In December, the first play written by Catherine McDonald, a graduate student from Chattanooga, Tennessee, *Close Quarters*, was presented on NBC's national television network in the Chevrolet Tele-Theatre, with Carolina's Sidney Blackmer playing the leading role.

Andy Griffith as Ko-Ko and Sam Hirsch as Poo-Bah in *The Mikado* (1948).

The tour play for 1948-49 was Sheridan's *School for Scandal*, enacted by James Geiger, Lynn Gault, Patricia Peteler, Hal Shadwell, Suzanne Davis (Mrs. Harry Davis), Estelle Ritchie, David Samples, Murray McCain, Marty Jacobs, and Claude Rayburn. And, in 1950, The Playmakers made a five-state tour with *Romeo and Juliet*, directed by Sam Selden, with Donald Treat as Romeo and Anne Martin as Juliet. The show encountered—and survived—a Mississippi flood.

Selden firmly believed that college theatres in the Southeast, with many similar interests and problems, should have an organization of their own. In this period the speech departments were flourishing in the Southeast. Most of the dramatic work in this area, however, was developing slowly in the shadow of Speech, under which it was commonly listed in the catalogues. Selden felt that Drama should be independent. He had been working toward that goal for several years. On March 4-5, 1949, directors from ten southeastern states were invited to Chapel Hill for a weekend devoted primarily to discussion of the theatre in the South.

Garrett Leverton of Samuel French, Inc., came down from New York to talk about "Broadway Today"; but other topics for discussion were "The Theatre in the South" and "The Negro in the American Theatre." Walter Prichard Eaton, critic and playwright, spoke on "The Regional Theatre: Its Opportunities and Responsibilities." Proff's son, Fred Koch, Jr., came up from Miami, Florida, to report on his "Theatre in the Round" experiences at the University of Miami.

After a spirited exchange of information and opinion, and some arguments, the Southeastern Theatre Conference was organized, with Kenneth Reardon of Duke University in Durham, North Carolina, the first president and John W. Parker of The University of North Carolina executive secretary.

Even the entertainment that weekend had a distinctively southern flavor: the visiting directors were invited to see the Playmaker production of Lillian Hellman's *The Little Foxes*, with Louise Lamont playing the role of Regina, which her cousin, Tallulah Bankhead, had played on Broadway. The cast also included Lillian Prince, Barbara McIntyre, Walter Creech, James

Geiger, A. E. Westover, III, and William MacIlwinen.

The year 1950 also had its highlights: *Medea* in the Forest Theatre with Marion Fitz-Simons in the title role (and there were friends in the audience who blanched when Medea was called upon to cast her son from the tower—the son being played by her own son, Michael Sean Fitz-Simons); *The Madwoman of Chaillot* with Lillian Prince; Paul Green's *Tread the Green Grass*, directed by Foster Fitz-Simons with music by the Pulitzer Prize-winning composer, Lamar Stringfield; and one of the all-time Playmaker hits, *Spring for Sure*, an original musical with book by Catherine McDonald, a graduate student, and music by Professor Wilton Mason of the Music Department.

Paul Green's early poetic fantasy, *Tread the Green Grass,* about the devastating effect of a narrow, fanatical religion on the soul of a young girl, was produced in Memorial Hall. Directed and choreographed with great sensitivity by Foster Fitz-Simons, it created unusual interest. Most of the adult audience, and many of the students, were moved by it; but some students, though admiring, were bewildered. The *Tar Heel* reported that "the audience was entertained though baffled. Whew!" In the cast were Anne Martin, Tommy Rezzuto, Elizabeth Savage, W. P. Covington, III, Gerald Honaker, and John Shearin.

Spring for Sure

Spring for Sure was a gay and lively show that both utilized the Playmaker folk play tradition and had fun with it at the same time. Bringing a plane full of sophisticated New Yorkers down in a remote valley of the Tennessee mountains, the play offered an opportunity for a comic confrontation between two very different worlds. The play was directed, acted, staged, and lighted by students—and was a tremendous success from the opening curtain, under the able direction of David Walter Morris.

Proceeds from the show went to the Koch Memorial Fund, established to develop and improve the Forest Theatre. Leading roles were played by Florabel Wolff, Lillian Prince, Catherine Covington, Lanier Davis, William Hardy, James Pritchett, and Sam Greene.

Lillian Prince in *The Madwoman of Chaillot* (1950).

Scene from the Playmaker production of the mountain musical, *Spring for Sure* (1950).

Popular songs from the musical included "Springtime in Tennessee," "Thar's Gold in Them Thar Hills," "It's Anglo-Saxon," "I'm Wild About Wild Life," and "Yaller, Yaller Moon."

In the spring of 1952, *Spring for Sure* was revived under John W. Parker's direction and was successfully taken on a four-week tour of eight states, from Virginia to Texas.

Other popular productions during these first years of Selden's regime included *Murder in the Cathedral* (with Fitz-Simons directing and Douglas Hume playing the lead); *Macbeth* with Sam Hirsch and Marion Fitz-Simons; *Rain* with Louise Lamont and Foster Fitz-Simons; and *Squaring the Circle* with Frank Groseclose, Edgar Loessin, and Larry Peerce. Groseclose later became a New York actor; Loessin is head of the drama department at East Carolina University; and Larry Peerce, son of Metropolitan Opera Star Jan Peerce, won acclaim as director of the motion pictures, *One Potato, Two Potato* and *Goodbye, Columbus.*

A new faculty member joined the staff of the department in 1950, Thomas M. Patterson, graduate of the University of Texas, with graduate work at Yale and Stanford. He took over the courses in playwriting and also directed numerous plays. His own play, *Monkey in the Moon*, was produced with considerable spirit by The Playmakers in 1954; and he later became the author of several outdoor dramas.

1951 Success Stories

In both academic distinction and public acceptance The Playmakers could note 1951 with considerable pride—and did.

A survey conducted by the Southern University Conference found The University of North Carolina second only to Johns Hopkins among southern colleges and universities in the number of liberal arts departments adjudged "among the best departments in the country." The Department of Dramatic Art was one of the ten North Carolina departments thus cited.

An Associated Press story out of Chapel Hill in October, 1951, made the surprising statement that during the previous year The Carolina Playmakers had attracted more people to their performances than Coach Carl Snavely's football team did to its. The score

Marion Fitz-Simons as Lady Macbeth (1947).

was: Carolina Playmakers — 440,000; UNC Football Team — 330,000. In short, drama had outdrawn football by 110,000! Such startling figures do require a bit of explanation. The football figures included attendance at all football games both in Chapel Hill and away from the campus. The Playmaker figures included the season's regular plays: *The Madwoman of Chaillot, Romeo and Juliet, Of Thee I Sing, The Druid Circle*, and *Caesar and Cleopatra*; a five-state tour of *Romeo and Juliet* to 23 towns and cities; and five outdoor dramas written or directed or both written and directed by Playmakers: *Unto These Hills* and *The Lost Colony* in North Carolina, *Forever This Land* in Illinois, *The Common Glory* in Virginia, and *Faith of Our Fathers* in Washington, D.C.

Even excluding the outdoor dramas, Sam Selden reported, Playmaker resident and touring productions outdrew the football team in the local Kenan Stadium by a score of 261,000 to 187,500.

Drama also attracted the University faculty that year; and nine popular faculty members played the nine Supreme Court judges in William MacIlwinen's production of the musical, *Of Thee I Sing*. They were E. J. Woodhouse, R. H. Wettach, Ernest Mackie, Joel Carter, John W. Parker, Samuel Selden, Walter Creech, W. H. Hartung, and Arthur Briskin.

Of course there had to be one dissenting note in such a flood of praise. It was also in 1951 that William Petersen, writing for the *Tar Heel*, complained that "folk drama has become so stereotyped that regionalism is often substituted for originality, dialect for dialogue and local problems for plot." He also declared that "a folk setting is beyond the experience of most audiences." He was commenting here not on the major public offerings of The Playmakers, but on the original writings of the students presented in their laboratory theatre work.

Offsetting such criticism is the 1951 letter written by Governor Adlai Stevenson of Illinois to University President Gordon Gray commending Samuel Selden and William MacIlwinen for the splendid work they had done in connection with the staging of Kermit Hunter's *Forever This Land* in Illinois. He described the

UNC faculty members as Supreme Court judges in *Of Thee I Sing* (1951).

two visiting Playmakers as "expert craftsmen as well as gentlemen of the highest type."

Koch Memorial Forest Theatre
The Forest Theatre was officially dedicated to Frederick Henry Koch on May 22, 1953. Soon after Proff's death, a campaign was started on campus by J. O. Bailey to raise funds for a new Koch Memorial Theatre but by 1946 only $3,602 had been raised so the plan was given up as impracticable and the money was used to improve the Forest Theatre with a new stone and timber dressing room and storage space behind the stage.

Former President Frank P. Graham gave the principal speech at the 1953 dedication and Archibald Henderson, now seventy-six, was Master of Ceremonies. Proff's granddaughter, Patricia Ann Koch, unveiled a plaque beside the entrance to the Forest Theatre that carried an inscription written by Dr. Henderson, one of Koch's closest friends through the years.

On the plaque Proff's students who had gathered for the ceremony could read: "The Forest Theatre — For here now under the greenwood tree in a new-world Forest of Arden through love and admiration of thousands of students is dedicated to Frederick Henry Koch — Born September 12, 1877 — Died August 16, 1944 — this open air palace of light and sound." Koch was fittingly described on the plaque as "an ardent genius who inspired and fostered the American folk play and like another Johnny Appleseed sowed the creative seeds of communal authorship throughout the American continent."

Sam Selden himself paid tribute to Proff with his brief biography, *Frederick Henry Koch: Pioneer Playmaker*, written with some help from Mary Tom Spanghos and published by The University of North Carolina Library in 1954.

New Full-length Plays
In spite of occasional doubts expressed by the *Tar Heel*, student playwriting flourished. Full-length original plays seemed to burst forth in Chapel Hill in the later 1940's and early 1950's. Not only were there Miss McDonald's *Spring for Sure* and Armstrong's

Egypt Lan', but 1949 saw productions of *Inherit the Wind* by
Gene A. McLain, *Repple Depple* by Sam Hirsch, and *The Spirit of
Cedarhurst* by Mildred Danforth, a Maine librarian who had come
to Chapel Hill ambitious to write a play—with ten dollars to last
two months and a willingness to babysit to earn the rest of what
she needed.

Four full-length original plays in 1950 must have set a record of
some sort: *Spring for Sure* had good company in successful pro-
ductions of *Angels Full Front* by Francis Michael Casey (cast
included Bruce Strait, Anne Martin, Josephine Sharkey, Elizabeth
Kearney, Charles Williamson, and Brad Arrington); *October in the
Spring* by Joseph G. Stockdale, Jr. (with Nat White, later to be
Richard Burton's stage manager in *Hamlet*, playing a retired
baseball player trying to make a comeback, supported by Sam
Greene, James Ginther, and Patricia Peteler); and *First String
Concerto* by Martha Nell Hardy. In 1951, came *Lo, the Angel* by
Nancy Wallace Henderson, *Tempest in a Teapot* by James Ginther,
and *Hospitality* by Jack Porter. Another full year was 1954 with
The Outsider by Emily Crow Selden (Mrs. Samuel Selden),
Darkening Shore by Kermit Hunter, and *Goodbye, Proud Earth*
by Mellrose Higginbotham. Mrs. Selden's play, directed by Kai
Jurgensen, has the unusual setting of Greek sponge fishing at
Tarpon Springs, Florida. The playwright even managed to find
several Greek students at the University to help provide authentic
details. In the cast were Tommy Rezzuto, Bill Trotman, Len
Bullock (who later toured with the road company of *No Time for
Sergeants*), Mary Helen Crain, and Bill Waddell with his guitar.

Professor Thomas Patterson's full-length comedy, *Monkey in
the Moon*, was produced in 1954, with Foster Fitz-Simons directing and an all-star Playmaker cast of the period: William Trotman,
Marion Fitz-Simons, Martha Nell Hardy, and Lloyd Borstelmann.
Chief roles in Kermit Hunter's play *Darkening Shore*, were taken
by Kai Jurgensen, Donnell Stoneman, Marian Rosenzweig, and
Lois Garren.

Additions to Staff
James Riley joined the staff as instructor in stage design and

technical direction in 1954 and remained until he went to New York in 1956. He was especially praised for the beautiful and imaginative production of *A Midsummer's Night's Dream* in the Forest Theatre in May, 1956.

Tommy Rezzuto, who had acted in so many Playmaker plays while an undergraduate, took over the designing job when Riley left and has also designed setting for such outdoor dramas as Kermit Hunter's *Horn in the West* and Paul Green's *The Stephen Foster Story*. Always popular among students, he had been elected to membership in the Order of the Golden Fleece as an under-graduate.

In 1958, Kai Jurgensen was awarded a Fulbright professorship to lecture in Denmark, where he also directed old Playmaker Agnar Mykle's *Morning in Yellow-Orange* for one of Copenhagen's professional theatres. Russell Graves joined the Dramatic Art faculty, coming from study at Carnegie Institute of Technology, Swarthmore, and Florida State and bringing a wide experience in radio and stage writing and directing. He was at one time playwright-in-residence at Dartmouth.

Forty-Year Celebration
The fortieth birthday of The Carolina Playmakers in 1958 celebrated the achievements of two of The Playmakers' most famous alumni: Paul Green and Thomas Wolfe, as well as pro-viding another pause to evaluate what the organization had accomplished.

In March, 1958, the University was host to the Southeastern Theatre Conference, which had been organized in Chapel Hill in 1949. Samuel Selden had served as president and Harry Davis would do so.

The feature of the conference was the presentation of eight of Paul Green's one-act plays, each given by a different producing group in the conference: *Supper for the Dead, Quare Medicine, Hymn to the Rising Sun, The Man Who Died at Twelve O'clock, The Last of the Lowries, Unto Such Glory, Fixin's,* and *The No 'Count Boy.*

Here, in two full evenings of drama, was the epitome of the

Carolina folk play. And at a dinner for conference delegates Paul
Green spoke on "Drama among the People."

Critic John Chapman of the *New York Daily News* was present
for the occasion, participated in a panel on "What Is the Future of
Regional Theatre?" and wrote an article for his paper when he
returned to New York.

"I go along with Paul Green," he wrote, "in believing that there
is no such thing as a deliberately regional theatre. There is only
theatre and if it is good, it will tell us something about the place
in which it is set."

He gave high praise to Paul Green, Thomas Wolfe, Proff Koch,
Samuel Selden, and such successful former Playmakers as Betty
Smith, Howard Richardson, Arnold Schulman, and Joseph Mitchell.
"The Broadway woods," he wrote, "are full of Southerners, of
course—actors, directors and technicians—for these Southeastern
states have a lively devotion to the theatre."

As for the plays he had just seen, he said: "Most effectively
staged was a biting, angry drama about a convict chaingang staged
by Selden himself, titled *Hymn to the Rising Sun*."

Pausing to look at their work on this fortieth birthday, The
Playmakers issued a brochure with an introductory note by
Chancellor William B. Aycock, in which he said: "Drama on the
campus of the University of North Carolina, now in its fortieth
year of life, is a glistening monument to the talented and hard-
working men and women who have given and are giving their lives
to the cultural growth of this state. The homespun quality of the
early folk plays taught students to write and, more importantly, to
face the realities of their environments and see them in truth and
beauty."

The brochure noted that the Department of Dramatic Art offered courses in the literature, history, and techniques of the
theatre; that the department offered three programs of study: a
Bachelor's Program to give a student a general liberal education,
a Master's Program to give more intensive literary and practical
training for a professional career, and a Licentiate's Program to
allow the holder of a Master's degree to develop a practical
specialty in directing, technical direction, playwriting, or theatre

administration; and that in forty years The Playmakers had presented at Chapel Hill more than nine hundred plays of all kinds, including more than seven hundred original scripts.

A forty-year Reunion Dinner at the Chapel Hill Country Club in May, 1958, brought back approximately one hundred Playmakers, including such old-timers as Jonathan Daniels, LeGette Blythe, Alga Leavitt, Cornelia Love, Aubrey Shackell, and Shepperd Strudwick and such more recent grads as Kermit Hunter, Josefina Niggli, Richard Adler, and Elmer Oettinger.

Look Homeward, Angel
To round off the celebration of forty years of activity, The Playmakers gave the first off-Broadway production of Ketti Frings's dramatization of Thomas Wolfe's *Look Homeward, Angel* in November, 1958, directed by Harry Davis in Memorial Hall twenty years after Wolfe's death. The occasion was steeped in nostalgia and the play itself characterized by especially good acting, with Robert Ketler playing young Eugene Gant (Thomas Wolfe) and Marion and Foster Fitz-Simons playing his parents, Eliza and W. O. Gant. Tommy Rezzuto played the dying brother, Ben. The reviewer for the *Chapel Hill Weekly* glowingly described the performance as "the outstanding local theatrical event of all time."

A "Wolfe Homecoming Dinner" at the Carolina Inn preceded the opening of the play, with Paul Green presiding and such guests present as Wolfe's sole surviving brother, Fred Wolfe of Spartanburg, South Carolina, and Mrs. Wolfe, President William Friday, Chancellor William B. Aycock, Victor Bryant of the Board of Trustees, Samuel Selden, and two of Wolfe's college roommates, Corydon Spruill and Albert Coates of the faculty.

Reminiscences of Wolfe's college days at Chapel Hill were given by Paul and Elizabeth Green, LeGette Blythe, and University Vice-president W. D. Carmichael, Jr.

Mr. Carmichael recalled Tom Wolfe's rushing late into Professor Edwin Greenlaw's English class one day and extracting from his pocket part of a roll of toilet paper, with typing on it, saying he had worked late the night before on his assignment and this was all the paper he could find.

Scene from *Look Homeward, Angel* (1958), with Tommy Rezzuto as Ben, Robert Ketler as Eugene Gant, Foster Fitz-Simons as W. O. Gant, and Marion Fitz-Simons as Eliza Gant.

Professor Greenlaw, unruffled, told him to read his paper. When he was halfway through, Greenlaw stopped him with: "I will observe from the quality of what you have written it is certainly typed on the right kind of paper."

LeGette Blythe remembered the same incident but added that this was just the sort of thing Tom Wolfe would do to get a laugh.

The regular work of The Playmakers was, or course, going right on under Selden, between celebrations. Playwright Lynn Riggs *(Green Grow the Lilacs)* visited the drama classes. And Charles Laughton, visiting the campus as director of *John Brown's Body*, with Tyrone Power, Judith Anderson, and Raymond Massey, told the students: "It seems to me that we and you people are the busiest theatre people in America today."

Hurricane and Goat
Occasionally The Playmakers had to contend with acts of nature. During the production of *The Crucible* in October, 1954, Hurricane Hazel tore the metal roofing off The Playmakers Theatre over the stage, but workers in the University Buildings Department saved the situation by tying ropes to themselves for protection against the wind and placing a tarpaulin over the hole so that the show could go on, to the relief of Director Fitz-Simons and his cast.

The running away of the goat which was a necessary character in *The Teahouse of the August Moon* in 1957 also might have been termed an act of nature, but fortunately the animal was recaptured by two young Chapel Hill boys and returned to the theatre to join the rest of the cast, including Ken Callender as Colonel Purdy, Joe Dillard as Captain Fisher, and Shawn Smith as Sakini.

There were a few unusual examples of casting, too, besides the goat. Also in *The Teahouse* was Sodsai Vanij-Vadhana of Bangkok, Thailand, as the pretty Lotus Blossom in this popular play of American-occupied Okinawa. Before returning to her native country, Sodsai spent several years in California. She saw her play, *Yankee, Don't Go Home,* produced at U.C.L.A. and she appeared on television. One of her memorable experiences was her attempt to teach Groucho Marx how to dance as an oriental.

And in *Mr. Roberts*, along with Tommy Rezzuto as Ensign Pulver and Donald Treat as Mr. Roberts, was a real-life Naval Commander cast as Naval Captain of the cargo ship. This was F. Lee Edwards, executive officer of the NROTC unit in Chapel Hill.

A special guest for the 1955 production of *Showboat* was Mrs. Beulah Adams Hunter, leading lady of the original Showboat (the James Adams Floating Theatre), where Edna Ferber did her research for the book. Mrs. Adams reminisced about her old showboat days and saw The Playmakers do their version under Kai Jurgensen's direction with John Shearin as Ravenal, Martha Fouse as Magnolia, David Small as Joe, Suzanne Elliot as Julie, Sidney Litwack as Andy Hawks, and Lillian Prince as Parthy.

New Original Plays
Successful productions were given of two full-length original plays: *Cat in Gloves* by Baxter Sasser and *Stranger in the Land* by Christian Moe, a drama of an American sailor (John Whitty) and his Japanese sweetheart (Nancetta Hudson). A production of *Dark of the Moon* by Howard Richardson and William Berney in the Forest Theatre featured Daniel Reed as the Witch Boy and Janet Carter as Barbara Allen.

The Playmakers also revived *Esther Wake*, an old 1919 melodrama by North Carolinian Adolphe Vermont, with Rusti Rothrock and Joe Whiteaker playing the leads.

Two popular plays taken on tour during this period were *The Rainmaker* in 1955, with James Heldman, James Sechrest, Louise Fletcher, and William Castevens, and Shaw's *Androcles and the Lion* in 1956 with John Whitty, Amanda Meiggs, John Sneden, Dick Newdick, and David Small. The Shaw play celebrated the centennial of Shaw's birth in 1856.

The Shakespeare tradition was continued with *The Tempest* in 1952 (Edgar Daniels was Caliban this time), *Julius Caesar* in 1955 (Walter Smith, Donald Treat, James Sechrest, Albert Gordon, Lloyd Skinner), *A Midsummer Night's Dream*, beautifully staged in the Forest Theatre in 1956 with Jane Albans as Titania, Dick Newdick as Puck, James Sechrest, Al Gordon, and Walter Smith,

James Sechrest, James Pritchett, and Louise Fletcher in *The Rainmaker* (1955).

and *The Comedy of Errors* in 1958, with the critical *Tar Heel* critic, Anthony Wolff, giving high praise to John Whitty, Darwin Solomon, Taylor Williams, John Sneden, and Amanda Meiggs.

Big musicals were *Kiss Me, Kate* in 1954 (Joel Carter and Jo Jurgensen played the leads; Tommy Rezzuto and William Hardy got great acclaim as the two gunmen singing "Brush Up Your Shakespeare"); *Brigadoon* in 1957 (John Sneden, Hope Sparger, Gene Strassler, and David Small); and *Oklahoma* in 1958 (with Lillian Prince, Darwin Solomon, Carolyn Myers, John Sneden, Margaret Starnes, and Fred Sitton drawing more applause than might be indicated by critic Wolff's decision that "the total result is poor").

Peer Gynt
Peer Gynt, in the translation by Kai Jurgensen and Robert Schenkkan, proved a Forest Theatre hit in 1957 under Jurgensen's direction, with Ken Lowry in the title role, supported by Amanda Meiggs and Martha Fouse. The opening night saw Governor Luther Hodges and University President William Friday in the audience and drew forth from critic Roy Moose the phrase "stunning production." He added, enthusiastically, that the play proved The Playmakers were "the most accomplished college acting group in the South, perhaps in the nation." Perhaps. At any rate, it was good to hear a critic speak so enthusiastically about a Playmaker production.

Many of the plays were familiar theatre pieces but were noted for outstanding performances: Fred Young in *The Inspector General*, Louise Lamont in *Lysistrata*, Marion Fitz-Simons in *Blood Wedding*, Amanda Meiggs in *The Lark*, James Sechrest and Julia Brown in *Seventeen*, Marion Fitz-Simons and Rusti Rothrock in *Anastasia*, Frank Groseclose and Virginia Michalak in *Caesar and Cleopatra*.

Other plays shared the acting plaudits more widely: *Darkness at Noon* (Fred Young, Larry Peerce, Hansford Rowe, Anne Edwards); *Winterset* (Frank Groseclose, Virginia Michalak, Kai Jurgensen, Elmer Oettinger); *Arsenic and Old Lace* (Marion Fitz-Simons, Eva McKenzie, who had played in old comedies with

Tommy Rezzuto and William Hardy singing "Brush Up Your Shakespeare" in *Kiss Me, Kate* (1954).

Charlie Chaplin and Ben Turpin, football quarterback Len
Bullock, novelist Manly Wade Wellman, Baxter Sasser, Albert
Gordon); and *Desire under the Elms* (Foster Fitz-Simons, Jo
Jurgensen, Albert Gordon).

Death of a Salesman, directed by Thomas Patterson in 1952,
was generally considered one of the best Playmaker performances
in years, with William Trotman as Willy, Mary Long as Linda,
Donald Treat as Happy, and James Pritchett as Biff. *A View from
the Bridge*, in 1958, also directed by Patterson, with Ken
Callender, John Sneden, Margaret Starnes, Al Gordon, Page
Williams, and Harvey Knox, drew from the usually carping *Tar
Heel* critic Wolff the statement: "For the first time in recent
productions there is something resembling a professional production on the Playmaker stage."

Samuel Selden's regime with The Playmakers at Chapel Hill was
coming to a close. He had revised the Dramatic Art curriculum and
had given the courses new academic strength. He had expanded the
old Playmaker writing of one-act Carolina folk plays to national
and international areas. He had encouraged a large number of full-
length plays by his students. He had organized the Southeastern
Theatre Conference and tied The Playmakers closer to the national
theatre scene. And with Selden, every member of the staff and all
the students were working productively.

Playmaker Alumni
Koch's old scrapbooks were bulging now with much new material
about Playmaker alumni. Such early Playmakers as Paul Green,
Jonathan Daniels, LeGette Blythe, Bernice Kelly Harris, and
Joseph Mitchell had written numerous books and plays. Frances
Gray Patton was author of the popular novel, *Good Morning, Miss
Dove*, and Josefina Niggli of *Mexican Village* and *Step Down,
Elder Brother*. Betty Smith had followed *A Tree Grows in
Brooklyn* with *Tomorrow Will Be Better* and *Maggie-Now*. Noel
Houston had written *The Great Promise* and Foster Fitz-Simons
Bright Leaf. Shepperd Strudwick was an established actor on the
stage, in the movies, and on television.

Younger Playmakers were also making their way. Andy Griffith

William Trotman as Willy Loman and Mary Long as Linda in *Death of a Salesman* (1952).

had played Will Stockdale in *No Time for Sergeants* and had made a movie, *A Face in the Crowd.* Robert Carroll had played in Jose Ferrer's production of *Cyrano de Bergerac*, had appeared as Gloria Swanson's lover in *Twentieth Century*, and had created the role of Lt. Mark Saber in ABC Radio's "Mystery Theatre." Douglas Watson had played Romeo to Olivia de Havilland's Juliet and appeared with Carol Stone in *Desire under the Elms*. Elizabeth Farrar had played in *The Cherry Orchard* and Christine White in *A Hatful of Rain*. Tom Avera had been in *Oklahoma* and in the Actors' Studio production of *Sundown Beach*. Porter Van Zandt had appeared in *Dial M for Murder*.

Robert Armstrong had played Big Daddy in *Cat on a Hot Tin Roof* and a leading role in *End as a Man*. Richard Adler had co-authored *Pajama Game* and *Damn Yankees*, in which Sam Greene and Charles Morrell appeared. Arnold Schulman had written *A Hole in the Head*, acted by Paul Douglas, Kay Medford, and Lee Grant. Howard Richardson's *Dark of the Moon* had made a hit in New York and on tour, with Playmakers Lillian Prince and Frances Goforth in the cast.

Whit Bissell had moved from Broadway to Hollywood and acted in such movies as *The Secret, Chicken Every Sunday, Lady in Ermine*, and *Quantrill's Raiders*. John Morgan was also in Hollywood and appeared in *Outrage, Fighter Squadron*, and Foster Fitz-Simons' *Bright Leaf*. Nananne Porcher was stage manager at New York City Center. Paul Nickell was directing plays on such top television programs as *Studio One* and *Playhouse 90*. James Pritchett, Estelle Ritchie, Sidney Shertzer, and Charles Williamson were acting on television, and Robert Dale Martin was casting director for CBS.

Growing Enrollment

Enrollment at the University was growing rapidly in the Selden period and this presented a new problem. From Koch's arrival in 1918 to his death in 1944, the number of students had increased only from 1,156 to 1,684; but in Selden's 15 years as department head, University enrollment had jumped to 7,959. It was more difficult for The Playmakers to remain a central part of the larger campus and not to be shut off as a small group of bohemian actors.

When Thomas Wolfe and Jonathan Daniels and Paul Green were the familiar Playmaker figures, other students were a small enough group to know them on the campus and recognize them on the stage. But as the student body grew larger, student activities became more compartmentalized, The Playmakers became more of a distinct group as they worked and played together around the theatre or at some favorite late-night eating spot downtown, and their fellow students began to point them out as "those Playmakers" rather than knowing them as individuals.

Constant gadfly-critic Anthony Wolff of the *Tar Heel* was not satisfied with the situation. Noting Selden's imminent departure, he called for "vital leadership and expansion of faculties, enrollment and curriculum" under the next department chairman.

"There is also a crying need to make the Playmakers an active part of Carolina life," he wrote, "both as an intellectual and educational stimulus and, equally important, as a source of entertainment." He noted that few students were attending the productions and that the department and the Playmaker group were drawing The Playmakers away from the rest of the students. The next fall he urged students to see the Playmaker shows and deplored the fact that of the 1,000 season tickets sold, so few had been purchased by students. Many students did, however, buy tickets to individual plays.

In January, 1959, Samuel Selden left the University to become head of the Department of Theater Arts at the University of California in Los Angeles. There he would succeed in setting up the Ph.D. phase of his "double pyramid" program which he had envisaged for North Carolina but had never been able to set up. His departure from Chapel Hill ended another chapter in the history of The Carolina Playmakers. Harry Davis took his place, first as acting chairman, then as chairman.

Commenting on Selden's achievements, an editorial in the *Charlotte News* said: "Selden has dutifully continued the tradition of the late Frederick H. Koch while expanding the technical features of the University program in dramatics. He initiated new undergraduate courses in theatre practice and supervised the development of graduate work in dramatic art. Under Selden, Chapel Hill became more and more a seedbed of original thought in the fields of dramatic technique and the esthetics of the theatre. Selden himself has written 10 books on the theatre."

Perhaps a fitting expression of Selden's contribution to The Playmakers in his years at their helm, an example of the gentle warmth beneath his determination to achieve excellence, may be seen in the affectionate recollection of a former Playmaker talking about Selden's encouragement of good playwriting: "Sam had listened to the reading of an angry, destructive play by a very earnest young playwright. Then he said, in that quiet way of his, 'But do you *like* any of the characters?'"

V. Harry Davis, 1959-1968

Harry Davis was, or course, no stranger to The Playmakers, but an intimate member of the family, having joined the staff in 1931, having acted and managed the tours in the 1930's, and having directed *Unto These Hills* at Cherokee. In 1939, he had taken a year's leave on a Rockefeller grant to secure his M.A. at Columbia University. When he took over the department in 1959, he fondly recalled sitting around Paul Green's living room and reading plays with Proff Koch, Sam Selden, and Betty Smith.

What were his plans for the future of The Playmakers?

"We want to preserve the traditions of the past," he said, "of the days of Thomas Wolfe and the other greats, but we also want to prepare ourselves for the new media and the new techniques. We expect to revise the curriculum. We may organize a repertory group and we may make the talent here available for international cultural exchange programs. We will prepare ourselves for the requirements of outdoor summer drama, for musicals, for television, for movies, and other media.

"We value and revere the folk drama and the regional plays, but we may also embark in new directions, for we may have a world market for drama."

In line with this thinking about his new assignment, Davis wrote to a friend in the summer of 1959:

Harry Davis, head of the Department of Dramatic Art, 1959-68.

The task at Chapel Hill is no easy one. In the past years our enrollment has been dropping gradually, especially in the undergraduate courses and, of course, we are greatly in need of a really adequate theatre plant. And we have been, to some extent, the victim of a reputation that we no longer can uphold—the era of the original folk play is gone with Proff Koch. But we can't live in the past. With a drive toward increasing our enrollment as a first objective, we've got to find some new and distinctive activity to carry on the name and fame of the group. The folk play has run its course, and the outdoor drama, as a prestige activity, has also begun to reach its crest. I have an idea that we might now, with the aid of some foundation funds, try to establish a fine repertory touring company, made up of our best graduates, for touring both at home and abroad. Coupling this with a new emphasis on new full-length plays, we might be able to find the legitimate "gimmick" that would carry us on in genuine progress.

There was no discernible change of direction that first year. The spring program included *The Would-Be Gentleman* (James Poteat, Arthur McDonald, Robert Ketler, Charles Nisbet, Betty Rhodes); *Mrs. McThing* (Louise Lamont, Frank McDonald, and Patricia Koch, Proff's young granddaughter); and *Inherit the Wind* in the Forest Theatre (Lloyd Borstelmann as Drummond-Darrow, Fred Sitton as Brady-Bryan, Robert Ketler as the schoolteacher, and John Sneden as the reporter—H. L. Mencken).

The fall of 1959 saw *Carousel* (Ethel Casey, Sally Pullen, Steve Kimbrough, Jr., Louise Lamont, John Sneden) and *A Little to the Left* (Robert Elston, Gordon Clark, Charles Nisbet, Bill File), followed in the spring of 1960 with *Volpone* (Kai Jurgensen, Isabella Davis, Darwin Solomon, Bob Merritt), *Summer and Smoke* (Shirley Dixon and Walter Lane Smith, III), *One More Waltz*, and *Oedipus Rex* and *Oedipus at Colonus* (with Foster Fitz-Simons playing the title role). Two of these plays were full-length originals: *A Little to the Left* by Brock Brower, a comedy of militarism in a "Banana Republic" which the reviewer considered a parody on Fidel Castro, and *One More Waltz* by Isabella Davis, wife of the director of The University of North Carolina Press, who had acted in numerous plays.

Two real hits came in the fall of 1960: *South Pacific* and Dylan Thomas' "Welsh play for voices," *Under Milk Wood*. Directed by Tom Patterson, *South Pacific* was described by *Tar Heel* critic Frank Murphy as "a theatre delight," with Professor Joel Carter as

DeBecque, Jane Page as Nellie Forbush, Marilyn Zschau as Bloody Mary, and Frank McDonald as Luther Billis. McDonald's belly dance with coconut shell breasts and a mop on his head brought down the house. The role of the native girl, Liat, was played by Elaine Chang, who fled China with her journalist father in 1950 after the Communists had taken over.

Under Milk Wood was directed by Foster Fitz-Simons, with sets by Lynn Gault, who had returned to the University for one year while Tommy Rezzuto was on leave to study at Northwestern. The student reviewer called it "a radical but rewarding departure" and gave high praise to its cast of William Trotman, Louise Lamont, Shirley Dixon, Lyla-Gaye van Valkenburgh, and Dorothy Silver.

The spring of 1961 moved on with *The Visit* (William Trotman, Mary Jane Webb, and football player Larry McMullen), which left the campus unimpressed; *Day of Glory*; and *The Great Diamond Robbery*, which was a lot of fun, with Susie Cordon as an enchanting villainess, Lynn Gault an appealing victim, Gordon Clark, Sally Pullen, Larry Steele, and Jack Hargett—and Romulus Linney contributing a brilliant olio act as an aging Shakespearean actor.

But let us look at *Day of Glory*, the American premiere of a play by the Danish playwright, Niels Locher, which was running simultaneously in Denmark at the Royal Theatre. Kai Jurgensen, of Danish birth himself, directed and had also translated the play.

The Playmakers made a real occasion of this premiere. American and Danish flags were displayed. The Danish Ambassador to the United States and the Lieutenant-Governor of North Carolina were present for opening night, as well as the University's Chancellor Aycock and Playwright Locher, who was presented a Playmaker Award. But this confused and confusing drama of the French Revolution was generally considered a disaster. "Day of Glory an inglorious night of theatre" said one reviewer, while another headlined "Glory Is Gory—All Soles without Soul." Even a cast which included Romulus Linney as Louis XVI, Jo Pettis as Madame Danton, William Trotman, and Byron Avery and the startling appearance of Napoleon Bonaparte with his hand stuck in his coat could not save the show.

Student Criticism

At this point restless students got in the act, not satisfied with where The Playmakers seemed to be going. Neil Clark was a *Tar Heel* reviewer almost as harshly critical as Anthony Wolff had been several years before. In September, 1961, he noted in the *Tar Heel:* "Some particularly harsh critics will say that the Playmakers have been living off an ancient reputation and haven't produced any original creative work since Professor Koch died. Although the actual situation is probably not so drastic, there is a definite point to such criticism. The Playmakers perhaps became sidetracked by the very thing that made them famous—folk drama and outdoor theatre."

In October, The Playmakers presented a well-received production of *The Matchmaker* and took it on tour in North Carolina and Georgia. Louise Lamont played the leading role, supported by John Crockett, halfback Larry McMullen, Dan Proctor, Vi Galvin, and Larry Randolph. They followed this with *The Beggar's Opera* in November, with Susie Cordon, Claudia Bray, Martha Teachey, Randolph Umberger, and Robert Williamson in the cast.

But, in January, 1962, the student *Tar Heel* was back on the attack, this time with a lead editorial headed "Mediocrity—or Possible Greatness." Referring to the late but most unlamented *Oedipus* as "something that would have caused Sophocles to steal a march from Socrates and take a belt of hemlock," the editor went on from there: "We are not asking that the Playmakers consciously try to neglect the people out front. Chapel Hill audiences are certainly sophisticated enough to appreciate more than an occasional dose of the off-beat, the imaginative and the original. . . . Sticking to standard stuff usually insures fairly good productions, but it also eliminates the possibilities of the once-in-a-lifetime brilliant production."

Except for the customary one-act original plays, which had not been exceptionally exciting during this period, the only Playmaker work that might have been considered "experimental" or "off-beat" had been the plays produced by such student organizations as the Student Theatre Workshop (organized in 1959) or the Petites Dramatiques (organized by the Student Union). These

groups produced *Waiting for Godot* in the fall of 1959, Camus'
The Misunderstanding in the spring of 1960, and Albee's *The
Sandbox* and *Zoo Story*. In the 1962-63 season, the two student
groups joined forces to present an exciting in-the-round production
of *The Miracle Worker* with actors and audience on the stage of
Memorial Hall. Wesley Van Tassell directed and Gordon Clark was
president of the Workshop at the time.

Two New Celebrations
The Carolina Dramatic Association celebrated its fortieth anniversary in the spring of 1962, when Governor Terry Sanford
proclaimed "State Drama Week in North Carolina," noting that
over the past forty years "the association has presented at its
annual State Drama Festival at the University in Chapel Hill, 1094
productions. Of these, 225 have been original plays by North Carolina playwrights, some of whom have since moved on to the
national scene. Thousands of young actors have raised their voices
in the venerable old Playmakers Theatre and have watched and
evaluated each other's work. Some of these have also gone on to
gain national recognition on the professional stage, in films or on
television."

As part of the celebration a dinner was held at the Carolina Inn,
with W. R. Taylor, first president of the association, as toastmaster
and Paul Green as festival speaker. Special recognition was given to
John W. Parker, director of the Bureau of Community Drama
since 1946; Mrs. Irene H. Fussler, executive secretary from 1931
to 1936; Mrs. Helen House, secretary and festival manager since
1952; and to the current officers: Josefina Niggli, president, and
John Sneden, vice-president.

Several plays presented by participating groups in the festival
were chosen to honor former Playmaker playwrights: *The Desert
Shall Rejoice* by Robert Finch, *Trail of Tears* by Elizabeth Welch
(author of ten award-winning festival plays), *Tooth or Shave* by
Josefina Niggli, *Rock Dust* by Mark R. Sumner, *Cottie Mourns* by
Patsy McMullan, *Shirt-Tail Boy* by W. P. Covington, III, *Leavin's*
by Janie Britt, *So Gracious Is the Time* by Betty Smith, and
Ca'line by Bernice Kelly Harris.

The Wilmington College Theatre also presented a cut version of *The Prince of Parthia* by Thomas Godfrey, the first play by an American author to be produced professionally in the U.S. Playwright Godfrey wrote the play in Wilmington, where he is buried. A history of the Carolina Dramatic Association (1922-62) was written by Harry Gene Lominac.

The next spring, in March of 1963, The Playmakers themselves celebrated another milestone: the 200th bill of new plays—and took another look at the past in a handsome brochure entitled *Adventures in Playmaking.*

A list of the one-act and full-length original plays produced by The Playmakers since that first *When Witches Ride*, in 1919, was published, with photographs from some of the plays; and Department Chairman Harry Davis contributed an excellent summary article entitled "How It All Began." His conclusion was:

> However distractive the political, social and scientific developments of our present day may be, the solution to its problems still lies with the individual, and the future belongs to the young.
>
> In celebrating that point in time when the Carolina Playmakers present their 200th bill of new plays, we look in two directions. With fondness and with pride we look backward over the 44 years of the past, in which 732 new one-act plays by students have come to life on our small stage, in which 46 new full-length plays have been produced there, and in which our colleagues in the Carolina Dramatic Association have presented there 225 new plays by their members. And with confidence and expectation we also look forward to the future, in which the insight and imagination of the new playwright, with the help of his fellow artists in the theatre, will continue to enrich, to enlighten, and to exalt our daily lives. As Mr. Koch would have said, "It has always been so."

The three new plays presented on this bill were *Pity Has a Human Face* by Scott Byrd, *Folly* by Wesley Van Tassel and *Clown for a Day* by Reginald Spaulding.

Special Student Night

Student leaders were still concerned that more students should see the Playmaker plays. In the fall of 1963, Pete Range and other students arranged with Department Chairman Harry Davis and Business Manager John W. Parker to establish a special "Student

Night" for the opening performance of new plays, with a student half-price of $1, instead of the customary $2. The *Tar Heel* also supported the plan, pointing out that during the previous year only fifty students had bought season tickets. All available student tickets were sold by the time of the second show, *Long Day's Journey into Night*, and the plan was considered a real success. The production of *My Fair Lady* in October, 1964, broke all Playmaker attendance records, with 5,379 tickets sold for the four performances, topping the previous record in 1958 of 4,571 for three performances of *Look Homeward, Angel*. Parker noted that of the 5,379 approximately 2,500 were UNC students and their dates. Students were obviously coming back to see The Playmakers —with a little encouragement.

Bachelor of Fine Arts
The most drastic new direction taken by The Carolina Playmakers during the Harry Davis chairmanship was undoubtedly the establishment of the B.F.A. (Bachelor of Fine Arts) program. This should also result in a noticeable change in the quantity and quality of training which can now be given to Dramatic Art majors.

Announcement was made in February of 1963 that a new Division of Fine Arts would be set up beginning with the fall of 1964 and including the Departments of Dramatic Art, Art, Music, and Radio-Television-Motion Pictures. Although women students had not previously been admitted to the University until their junior year, twenty-four freshmen women were admitted in the fall of 1963, six of them planning to major in Dramatic Art. Three of these would become Playmaker leading ladies in the plays of 1967 and 1968: Virginia Cornue, Laurel Dykstra, and Anne Peacock. All girls became eligible for admission application to the University in the fall of 1964.

Under this new B.F.A. program all Dramatic Art majors would take four courses in Dramatic Art each semester of their freshman year (Acting, Technical Methods, Voice Training, and Stage Movement) in addition to required freshman courses in English, foreign languages, and physical education.

During the sophomore, junior, and senior years, the student could choose either the "acting option" or the "design-technical option" and take approximately fourteen additional courses in Dramatic Art and the remaining sixteen courses from required and elective courses in the College of Arts and Sciences.

New additional dramatic scholarships were also set up: a $1,000 scholarship given by the William Morris Agency and a $2,500 Shubert Fellowship in Playwriting, awarded for the first time to Randolph Umberger.

Visitors to Campus
Guests on the campus from the professional theatre during this period included Dore Schary, a director-producer-writer, who was Artist-in-Residence for a week and worked closely with Dramatic Art students; Richard Corson, author of a definitive book on stage make-up, who conducted a make-up seminar class; Robert Dale Martin, casting director for CBS television, who talked about television acting; Lee Simonson, New York designer, who gave a series of lectures at The Playmakers Theatre and a public lecture on "Eugene O'Neill as a Dramatist"; John Frankenheimer, director, whose lecture on "Popular Misconceptions of Television" was sponsored by the Carolina Forum; Eric Salmon, British actor and director, who was visiting professor in Dramatic Art and Radio-Television-Motion Pictures and staged a local television production of Pirandello's *Six Characters in Search of an Author*, with a number of Playmakers in the cast; and Franchot Tone, stage and film actor, who talked to D.A. classes and made a television tribute to Shakespeare, with Eric Salmon and his wife, Janet Crowder.

New Full-Length Plays
Original full-length plays produced in the 1960's included *Renegade* by Carl Hinrichs, a play of the Civil War which found critics unenthusiastic except for a tranquilized rabbit and the ballads of Sandy Moffat; *Marriage Wheel* by Joel Climenhaga, a play about an arranged marriage among the Pennsylvania Dutch, written by a visiting professor replacing Tom Patterson, who had a

Fulbright professorship to Korea; *The Summer Tree* by Randolph Umberger, a tender play of adolescence and innocence; and *The Battle of the Carnival and Lent*, an ambitious drama about the Middle Ages by Professor Russell Graves.

The Summer Tree had been successfully performed as a one-act play before playwright Umberger converted it into a full-length. Umberger is considered one of the most promising playwrights of the present student generation; and his new play, *Amen to a Mantis*, which was performed on Long Island with Patricia Neway in a leading role, was selected for Chapel Hill production as part of the fifty-year celebration. The production of Professor Graves' play was reviewed by Henry Hewes, drama critic for *Saturday Review*, who discussed with drama and reviewing students how he reviewed a new drama.

In February, 1964, The Playmakers presented *The Busy Martyr* by George Hitchcock, the current play-of-the-year selection of the Southeastern Theatre Conference, which encouraged its members to produce a selected original play to help support promising new playwrights.

Hits of the 1960's
Since the 1950's the major productions of The Playmakers had been attracting sell-out audiences and usually had to be held over for extra performances. O'Neill's *Long Day's Journey into Night,* directed by Tom Patterson in November, 1963, brought rave reviews for the quality of acting by its principals: Marion Fitz-Simons, Earl Wynn, Frank McDonald, and Richard Parks, but its audiences were distracted and distressed by the assassination of President Kennedy during the run of the play.

Archibald MacLeish's *J. B.*, directed by Harry Davis in the winter of 1964, brought back in the leading role David Hooks, a former Playmaker who had made a reputation in New York for his roles in *Inherit the Wind, Gideon, The American Dream,* and *Zoo Story*. While Hooks was on the campus for three weeks of rehearsal, he also was guest lecturer in various drama classes. Playing supporting roles were Foster Fitz-Simons, Martha Nell Hardy, and David Gullette.

John Whitty as Professor Henry Higgins in *My Fair Lady* (1964).

Unsurprisingly, *My Fair Lady* in October, 1964, was a great
favorite of the students and broke all Playmaker attendance
records. Under the direction of Tom Patterson and with stunning
sets by Tommy Rezzuto and costumes by Irene Rains, the show
featured John Whitty as Henry Higgins, Peggy Jones as Eliza
Doolittle, Fred Cook as Alfred P. Doolittle, Graham Pollock, Jo
Pettis, and Anne West. The *Tar Heel's* enthusiastic comment was
"smashing lively production."

Oscar Wilde's *The Importance of Being Earnest* in March, 1966,
directed by Tommy Rezzuto, turned out to be a particular pleasure for the audience, which admired not only the period sets and
costumes but also the period acting of Amanda Meiggs, Carolyn
Fitz-Simons, Tom Hull, James Slaughter, and Louise Lamont.

Chekhov's *The Three Sisters* in March, 1967, directed by Mark
Schoenberg, was the play that perhaps best illustrated how much
the new Bachelor of Fine Arts program could enhance the quality
of Playmaker shows. Cast almost entirely from B.F.A. students
(Virginia Cornue, Laurel Dykstra, Kristine Hoover, Chris Parsons,
Douglas Barger), the play was also given nearly twice the rehearsal
time of most Playmaker shows and, as a result, had much greater
depth of characterization than had usually been possible.

Brendan Behan's *The Hostage* in May, 1968, came nearest to
answering the current student request for more offbeat, contemporary drama and proved very popular with most of the
audience—but shocking and bewildering to some segments. The
play was directed by Foster Fitz-Simons and Mark Schoenberg and
was considered an exciting "happening" by enthusiastic students
and reviewers.

Another hit of this period was *The Fantasticks*, directed by
student Larry Warner in March, 1964, as a "special added attrac-
tion" and still talked about for the outstanding performance of
John Whitty, Roberts Batson, Tom Hull, Graham Pollock, Anne
Peacock, and Richard Parks.

Two of the more contemporary and offbeat plays of the period
were Ionesco's *Rhinoceros* in 1963, acted by John Crockett, Larry
Warner, and Juanese Hatton, and taken on tour through North
Carolina and Georgia; and Kopit's *Oh, Dad, Poor Dad* in February,

Chekhov's *The Three Sisters* (1967), with Laurel Dykstra, Virginia Cornue, and Kristine Hoover.

Brendan Behan's *The Hostage* (1968) with (reading clockwise from top) Roger Howell, Ian O'Connell, Walter Smith, Madge Bunce, Hitoshi Sato, Linda Earp, Kristine Hoover, Pat Hurley, Tom Kindle, and Jean Marie Blair.

1965, when the local reviewer found that "the cast milked meaning from the absurd" (Martha Nell Hardy, Michael Carrington, George Gray, and Sara Kravitz).

The production most nearly resembling the first Playmaker plays of the 1920's was *Tobacco Road* in November, 1962, when over half a ton of real dirt was hauled onto the Playmaker stage to match the "realism" of Lloyd Borstelmann as Jeter Lester, Dan Proctor as Dude, Betty Setzer as Sister Bessie, Susie Cordon as Ada, and Mary Lindsay Spearman as Pearl. The *Tar Heel* proclaimed "The Hicks Click."

One of the most exciting evenings of the 1960's was the opening night of *The Chalk Garden*, when the two "first ladies of the Playmaker Stage," Marion Fitz-Simons and Louise Lamont, appeared for the first time in the same play on the Playmaker stage. Members of the audience aware of the situation were so intent on seeing who would upstage whom and how that they could hardly notice the rest of the cast, which included Jo Pettis, Graham Pollock, Larry Randolph, and Mary Lindsay Spearman.

Leading Players

As emphasis on the original one-act plays had decreased during the Selden-Davis years, the focus was naturally on the full-length original plays and on the five or six professional plays given each season. An interested audience could still be gathered for an evening each semester of student-written-and-directed one-acts; and spirited discussion, led by a staff member, still followed each play. But the publicity, the build-up and the attention were now in other areas.

Some of the other major plays of the period and the actors who played leading roles were: *Dr. Faustus* (Gordon Clark), *Only in America* (Kai Jurgensen as Harry Golden, but the reviewer complained of the choice of the play—"Playmakers have sold out"), *The Braggart Soldier* (Graham Pollock), *Hamlet* (David Gullette was praised in the title role but the reviewer declared: "The present production of *Hamlet* is a real tragedy"), *Billy Budd* (Chris Parsons), *A Streetcar Named Desire* (Amanda Meiggs and Bill Smith), *Finian's Rainbow* (James Slaughter), *Holiday Mountain*

(James Boothby), and *The Trojan Women* (Martha Nell Hardy). *The Cherry Orchard* was dismissed as "cold turkey."

New Staff Additions
Two new staff members joined the faculty of the Department of Dramatic Art in 1966: Mark Schoenberg, who took his B.F.A. at Carnegie Institute of Technology and his M.F.A. and Ph.D. at Tulane University and has taught, acted, and directed in New York and elsewhere; and Joseph Talarowski, who studied at the University of Delaware and the University of Denver, where he received his Ph.D., and at the Institute for Advanced Studies in New York.

Newcomers to the staff in 1967 were Patricia Barnett, with degrees from the Catholic University of America and the University of Denver, who teaches stage speech; and Jack Shirk, who comes to UNC from Kansas State, Oklahoma City University, Purdue, and Texas Christian and teaches stage lighting. Miss Barnett's direction of *The Chinese Chalk Circle* in 1968 marked the first direction by a woman of a major Playmaker production.

The fall of 1968 brought two additional members to the staff: John Christopher Whitty from the University of Iowa, a graduate of UNC now completing his work for a Ph.D. and an expert in business management; and Clark McCormack Rogers, who has a Ph.D. from Louisiana State University and is a specialist in dramatic literature and research.

New Building
Throughout the years of Harry Davis' chairmanship all the Playmaker staff had fully realized the desperate need for a new theatre building. This was, of course, no new realization. As early as 1944, in the Koch Memorial Issue of the *Carolina Play-Book*, Professor Selden had expressed the needs in an article, "A Dramatic Art Building," in which he stated:

> The activities of the Playmakers have grown so extensively in the years since their inception that the present building cannot now hold more than a small part of them. The office of the Director, the Dramatic Museum, the Business Office, the Bureau of Community Drama, the Radio Studio,

the Scene Shop, the Costume Shop, and the several store rooms are located in seven different places on and off the campus—all of them outside the theatre and most of them at a considerable distance from it. The University classes in Dramatic Art have trouble finding adequate room for laboratory work, and directors are constantly hunting for spots in which to hold their rehearsals.

Selden then described a desired new theatre building, which the staff had been planning since 1936. Actual floor plans were drawn up by Waldron Faulkner, a Washington architect; and a site was picked out just east of the Bell Tower on a wooded lot across from the University Library. But in the subsequent years sufficient funds were never available from the University and the State Legislature, so the dream remained only a dream—and The Playmakers did the best they could do with their inadequate and scattered facilities.

In the recent years, new plans have been drawn and new efforts have been made to secure funds. In the summer of 1964, a new theatre to cost $1,245,000 was requested by the University of the Legislature as part of a permanent improvements item for the 1965 budget. The theatre was placed in tenth position on the list of University requests, which was headed by a new Law Building. Dean of Faculty James L. Godfrey declared that unless the theatre request was granted, "the Dramatic Art Department will be condemned to moribund gentility."

The theatre has still not been authorized, although the new Law Building was opened for occupancy in the fall of 1968. The University requests to the 1967 Legislature and again to the 1969 session had a new theatre high on the list of desperately needed buildings. Thus far the Legislature has not been responsive to the request.

In recent months new plans have been worked on by Charlotte architect A. G. O'Dell, in consultation with George Jenkins, New York theatre designer and engineer, for presentation to the Legislature. The proposed building would contain about 80,500 square feet and include an auditorium seating 600. Estimated cost of the structure is $3,000,000.

Part of the $200,000 bequest to The Playmakers from the late Lillian Prince, who died February 25, 1962, was used to pay for the plans. Mrs. Prince had been very active with The Playmakers while she and her husband, the late William Meade Prince, artist and illustrator, lived in Chapel Hill. Among the plays in which Mrs. Prince had leading roles were *Ah, Wilderness, Spring for Sure, The House of Connelly,* and *Oklahoma!*

In 1969, Playmaker staff members are hopeful that the next fifty years will find them in more adequate quarters than they enjoyed during the first fifty years!

In the meantime, the University has turned over Graham Memorial, the old Student Union Building, to The Playmakers and the Department of Dramatic Art. Use of Graham Memorial will allow The Playmakers to house most of their activities under one roof—for the first time in history. The main lounge can be used for plays and other rooms used for experimental plays and rehearsals. There is also space for classrooms, costume shop, business office, Bureau of Community Drama, Institute of Outdoor Drama, and offices for all staff members.

Playmaker Alumni

During the years of Harry Davis' chairmanship the old Koch scrapbooks continued to expand with clippings of the activities of former Playmakers now out in the professional theatre world.

Both Shepperd Strudwick and George Grizzard acted in New York in Edward Albee's *Who's Afraid of Virginia Woolf?* Andy Griffith and Whit Bissell continued their work in television and motion pictures. Douglas Watson acted with Faye Dunaway in *A Man for All Seasons*, with Zoe Caldwell and his own daughter in *The Prime of Miss Jean Brodie*, had the title role in *Richard III* at the Stratford, Connecticut, Shakespeare Festival—and picked up along the way the New York Critics Variety Poll Award, the Clarence Derwent Award, and the Theatre World Award for his acting.

James Pritchett was understudy to Hal March in *Two for the Seesaw*, when Porter Van Zandt was stage manager, and has played a leading role for a number of years in the popular television show, *The Doctors*. David Hooks appeared in *Zoo Story* and in Ugo Betti's *Corruption in the Palace of Justice.* Amanda

Meiggs was in an off-Broadway revival of *The Young and the
Beautiful;* and Hal England toured as the star of *How to Succeed
in Business without Really Trying.*

Shepperd Strudwick came to the Durham Star Playhouse in *Mr.
Roberts* and Edgar Daniels as Big Daddy in *Cat on a Hot Tin Roof.*
Daniels also appeared in New York in *Caligula.* Louise Fletcher
appeared in a Playhouse 90 television show, *The Last Man*, and in
other spots on *Bat Masterson, Lawman, Maverick*, and *Yancy
Derringer.*

One CBS television program, *Look Up and Live*, had three ex-
Playmakers in the cast: Betsy Farrar Thurman, Eugenia Rawls, and
Mary Lindsay Spearman—and Playmaker Bruce Minnix directed
and Robert Dale Martin was in charge of casting.

And in the fall of 1968, news clippings from New York announced the opening of a new musical, *Noel Coward's Sweet
Potato*, starring George Grizzard; and two new motion pictures
with scripts written by Arnold Schulman, *Star Spangled Girl* and
Goodbye, Columbus (directed by Larry Peerce).

Fifty-Year Celebration
The year 1968-69 marks the fiftieth anniversary of The Carolina
Playmakers—and they spent the preceding year planning to celebrate it. Sam Selden, who succeeded Proff Koch as director of The
Playmakers and chairman of the Department of Dramatic Art,
returned to Chapel Hill after retiring as department head at the
University of California at Los Angeles and was asked to be
coordinator of the celebration. Invitations went out to approximately 6,000 Playmaker alumni, urging them to come home and
help celebrate.

The season's program of plays was built around the celebration,
with four major productions scheduled for Memorial Hall and the
Forest Theatre: a musical, *The Most Happy Fella*, in October;
Anouilh's *Becket* in November; a new play by Paul Green, *Sing All
a Green Willow*, in March; and Shakespeare's *The Taming of the
Shrew*, a revival of the first Playmaker play in the Forest Theatre,
in May.

In addition, three productions were announced for The Play-

makers Theatre: *Encore!* in December, *Amen to a Mantis* in
February, and *Thirty-Seven Octobers* in April.

The *Encore!* program was advertised as "three of the best origi-
nal one-act plays from the Playmakers' treasury": Josefina Niggli's
Mexican comedy, *Tooth or Shave* (1936); Gwen Pharis
Ringwood's Canadian drama, *Still Stands the House* (1938); and
Wallace Johnson's more recent play, *What Did You Learn in
School Today?* (1962). Oddly enough, for a fifty-year celebration,
not one of the famous early plays on which the Playmaker
reputation was founded was included, such as *When Witches Ride,
Fixin's,* or *Quare Medicine.*

Amen to a Mantis is a new full-length original play by Randolph
Umberger, author of the successful *The Summer Tree*, and is a
drama set on the quaint offshore North Carolina island of
Ocracoke. *Thirty-Seven Octobers* is "a dramatic interpretation and
staging of selections from the work of Thomas Wolfe, arranged by
C. Hugh Holman, renowned authority on the writer."

A series of lectures was also scheduled for the year: Sir Tyrone
Guthrie in November, playwright Robert Anderson in February,
and critic Howard Taubman in March.

The climax of the Golden Year festivities was to be the reunion
dinner in March, when all Playmaker alumni of the past fifty years
would be invited to attend a banquet, a Capers program, a panel
program of celebrities discussing some lively theatre topic, and a
performance of Paul Green's play.

Death of Harry Davis

Just prior to the beginning of the fifty-year Celebration, which he
had helped plan and looked forward to enjoying as it would bring
back so many Playmakers with whom he had worked from 1931
to 1968, Harry Ellerbe Davis died on September 15, 1968.

During his nine years as chairman, the Department of Dramatic
Art and The Carolina Playmakers had built up a strong and steady
attendance at plays, usually with sellout crowds, had continued a
busy program of writing and producing new one-act and full-
length plays, had inaugurated the ambitious B.F.A. program,
which would give its students an intensive four-year period of

Patricia Barnett, Clark Rogers, and Malcolm Groome in *Amen to a Mantis* (1969).

training, and had widened its strong support of outdoor dramas across the country by establishing the Institute of Outdoor Drama. Director of *Unto These Hills*, the outdoor drama at Cherokee, North Carolina, since its beginning in 1950, Davis saw that show pass the 2,250,000 mark in attendance, a figure which made it the most popular outdoor drama in the country.

Harry Davis had recognized, just as Sam Selden had, the inevitable conflict in any drama department between adequate professional training and broad liberal arts background. He expressed his thinking in this area in some of his books and public speeches.

In the introduction to his book, *Stage Lighting*, he defined the theatre as "primarily an art endeavor, the place where man, in the company of his fellows, observes and studies himself—his own individual and collective joys and sorrows."

And speaking to the Philological Club in 1967 on "Academic Discipline for the Performing Artist," Davis discussed the training he believed a professional actor should have to perform effectively in a theatre.

Obviously body-training and voice-training are fundamental and basic needs since an actor must use himself as the instrument of his art. . . . But above and beyond this intensive technical training, the actor needs equally as urgently, in my opinion, to train his mind. . . . The professional actor needs a good liberal education, in the usual sense of that term, in addition to his specialized training. This should logically be given in the mainstream of existing public education. Appropriately, his education will fall within the humanistic areas. For a liberalizing education looks outward toward other arts, sciences and humanities, and provides a broad base on which specialized training can rest.

It develops qualities of mind that are as valuable to the actor, and as important to him, as to any other human being: curiosity about the world and its universe, a responsiveness to beauty of all kinds, a willingness to live some part of one's life with serious ideas, an ability to see life honestly, and to see it whole. And the most effective period in which basic professional training can be given is between the ages of 17 and 25—the period approximately during which the liberalizing education is best provided.

He suggested that, as in the education of doctors, lawyers, and other professional specialists, the greater weight should be given to the liberal and broader studies in the early part of the college program and to the professional training in the later period of study.

Though he thought and spoke frequently about the quality of theatre training that could be given at the University, Davis devoted much of his time and attention to the summer outdoor dramas, which he saw as an extension of University training and which had attracted him since he first directed *Unto These Hills* at Cherokee in 1950.

Contributing an article on "Outdoor Drama: A Mainstream of Mankind" to the 1968 program for *Unto These Hills*, Davis compared the outdoor dramas to the old Greek theatre.

> Generally speaking, when theatre played outdoors, it was a vehicle of the people, giving immediate expression to their fundamental hopes, fears and ambitions. Moved indoors, theatre became a toy of the nobility and the rich, or a mental exercise of self-contained intellectuals. Basically, this is the type of "professional" theatre today.
>
> We are in a process of search for newer forms of expression, forms that might more clearly express the frenetic complexities of present-day society. Unhappily, these new presentations rarely appeal to the spiritual side of their audiences, but tend to be downbeat, to emphasize the lost condition of mankind rather than the uphill battle against this so-called "hopelessly lost" condition. In a society that seldom has any more strongman heroes, drama also has drifted away from the story of single individuals battling against fate. Instead, we are presented with sad, rather forlorn souls, stranded in an environment not of their making, without direction, without trust, without love. Theatre has once again lost its great spiritual appeal to the common man.

This strong conviction of Harry Davis about what theatre should be and his equally strong dislike for what he called "the currently popular attitude of nihilism and defeatism" and "small stories about small people" in the modern theatre may have influenced, during his years as department head, the "sticking to standard stuff" criticized by the *Tar Heel* and other students who were asking for more "off-beat, imaginative and original" theatrical fare.

When Harry Davis assumed the department chairmanship in 1959, he spoke of "preserving the traditions of the past" but he also suggested the possibility of revising the curriculum, of organizing a repertory company, and of making talent available for an international cultural exchange program. "We will prepare ourselves for the requirements of outdoor summer drama, for musicals, for television, for movies and other media," he said.

Establishment of the B.F.A. program did, of course, involve revising the curriculum. And certainly the department made many of its students available for the various summer outdoor dramas. But the proposed repertory company never materialized; and there was no further mention of an "international cultural exchange program." Any work done for movies or television remained primarily in the Department of Radio-Television-and-Motion Pictures; and there was little co-operation between the two departments.

Davis had inherited a staff of old friends and fellow workers who knew each other and had worked together warmly and well; but it was a department that had been operating democratically rather than autocratically. Everybody had his say about what should be done and how it should be done. In the selection of plays, each staff member had his own favorite that he would like to direct. There was also a difference of opinion about how flexible or rigid the new B.F.A. program should be, whether B.F.A. freshmen should be allowed to act in plays, and whether all plays should be cast from B.F.A. students or from a wider range of other students and adult actors in the community.

When the frustrations of operating a "democratic" department bore in too heavily upon him, Harry Davis tended to turn more and more to the rewarding work of directing the summer outdoor drama, *Unto These Hills*, where he had complete authority and fewer frustrations and where he could also look around the Cherokee community and see the very satisfying results of what the show had done for the people and the economic welfare of the town. As for the Department of Dramatic Art and The Carolina Playmakers, he was already looking forward to his retirement as department chairman after the strenuous chore of celebrating in an appropriate manner the fifty-year anniversary in 1968-69.

VI. The Fifty-Year Anniversary

Enthusiastic plans for the fifty-year anniversary celebration throughout 1968-69 were dampened by the death of Department Chairman Harry Davis, but Acting Chairman Thomas Patterson and his staff members, with the experienced aid of former Chairman Samuel Selden, set up the year's program as Davis had envisioned it.

Three of the plays selected for production during the year were the *Most Happy Fella, Becket,* and *The Taming of the Shrew,* offset somewhat by a new Paul Green play, *Sing All a Green Willow,* and a new Randolph Umberger drama of a fisher family on Ocracoke Island, *Amen to a Mantis.*

The bill that revived three old Carolina folk plays, *Encore,* was expected to be a highlight of the celebration but turned out to be what one student critic termed "a disaster." Josefina Niggli's *Tooth or Shave* (1936) and Gwen Pharis Ringwood's *Still Stands the House* (1938), although selected as two of the best folk plays from earlier days, found lukewarm response from the 1968 audience. Only the 1962 *What Did You Learn in School Today?* by Wallace Johnson, directed by Clark Rogers with a sharp eye for

Thomas Patterson, acting chairman of the Department of Dramatic Art since 1968.

movement and pace, aroused any enthusiasm. The lackluster production and cool reception for *Encore* may indeed have finished off the old dependence upon the one-act folk play as the once staple Playmaker product.

Another highlight of the fiftieth anniversary was to have been a November lecture on the state of the theatre today by Sir Tyrone Guthrie, founder of the Stratford, Ontario, Shakespeare Festival and the Guthrie Theatre in Minneapolis. Unfortunately for the University students, townspeople, and bus-loads of drama students from surrounding towns who filled Hill Hall to hear Guthrie, he had delivered his talk on contemporary theatre to drama students in the afternoon and gave his evening audience only a program of readings from Irish poets and short story writers. This was partially compensated for when playwright Robert Anderson, author of *Tea and Sympathy* and *You Know I Can't Hear You when the Water's Running*, gave a brilliant and witty address on "The Future of the American Playwright" at The Playmakers Theatre in February.

An engaging feature of the year was provided by former Playmaker Eugenia Rawls, who visited the campus in January and gave "An Evening with Fanny Kemble," based on the memoirs and letters of the famous nineteenth-century English actress who visited the United States and married a southern planter.

The fall production of *Becket* had brought two Playmaker alumni back to the campus to star in the leading roles: David Hooks and Gordon Fearing. William Trotman returned to portray Thomas Wolfe in the Hugh Holman edited "readings" from Wolfe's work entitled *Thirty-Seven Octobers*, and James Sechrest returned to play the juvenile lead in Paul Green's *Sing All a Green Willow*.

Climaxing the fifty-year anniversary was the Playmaker Reunion March 27-29, which brought back to the campus several hundred alumni, including Sidney Blackmer, Paul and Elizabeth (Lay) Green, LeGette Blythe, Frances Patton, Hubert Heffner, Lee Elmore, Jane Toy Coolidge, Mary Yellott McNitt, Wilbur Dorsett, Howard Bailey, Bill and Mary Long, Fred Howard, Howard Richardson, Bob du Four, Robert Dale Martin, Josefina Niggli, Frank Durham, Lynn Gault, Gwen Pharis Ringwood, Richard Adler,

Nananne Porcher, Sam Hirsch, and Fred Young. Playmakers who had acted together in Chapel Hill over the years sought out their own contemporaries and gathered in corners of Graham Memorial or the Carolina Inn to talk over old times.

A dinner at the Holiday Inn on Friday evening was a highlight of the weekend, with some Capers-like skits (Bill Hardy and Tommy Rezzuto singing "Brush Up Your Shakespeare") and informal reminiscences from any Playmakers who felt like recalling the past.

A Saturday morning panel discussion focused the attention of the alumni on "College Training: Help or Hindrance to a Professional Theatre Career?" Participants were alumni Robert Dale Martin, Sam Hirsch, Nananne Porcher, and old Playmaker friend Norris Houghton.

On Saturday afternoon Paul Green gathered the Playmaker alumni into The Playmakers Theatre for what turned out to be almost an old-fashioned revival meeting, with enthusiastic suggestions about securing the desperately needed new theatre. Alumnus Richard Adler led the discussion and pledged $75,000 himself toward a new building. Other alumni promised to help in fund raising and to write members of the North Carolina Legislature asking for State funds for a building.

Saturday evening the whole group of returning Playmakers took in the production of Paul Green's *Sing All a Green Willow*, which might be described as "a satiric folk fantasy" based on an earlier Green play, *Tread the Green Grass*. Samuel Selden directed with James Sechrest imported from the ranks of professional alumni as a young mountain boy, Joel Carter from the Department of Music as an evangelist, and most of the other actors current student Playmakers.

There was a mood of excitement in the audience and as the play unfolded, many Playmakers felt they could indeed "go home again" for they glimpsed characters on the stage reminiscent of earlier Green plays and of familiar Playmaker themes. But, just as in the case of *Encore* earlier in the season, there was a restive feeling that the old ways and old plays were not relevant to today's new audiences. Reviewing the play in *The Chapel Hill Weekly*,

Carol Case Erskine and Joel Carter in Paul Green's *Sing All a Green Willow* (1969).

Playmaker William Hardy expressed his respect and admiration for Green, "a giant among us merely mortal men," but lamented the play as "nothing more than a bloodless ghost of a glorious past."

Sing All a Green Willow was an interesting and perhaps worthwhile experimental production of satire-and-fantasy and it epitomized many of the Playmaker strong points in producing native drama through the years; but its attempt to dramatize the old theme of the disastrous effect of fanatical southern religion on young people turned out to be dated and seemed scarcely pertinent to the problems of today.

Randolph Umberger's *Amen to a Mantis*, directed by Tommy Rezzuto, and Shakespeare's *The Taming of the Shrew*, directed by Kai Jurgensen in the Forest Theatre, drew more favorable reviews. Ken Ripley in the *Tar Heel* called *Amen* "the most meaningful and stimulating presentation produced this year by the Playmakers." And William Hardy, reviewing *The Taming of the Shrew* for *The Chapel Hill Weekly*, gave special praise to Roger Howell as Petruchio, Margaret Howell as Kate and Haskell Fitz-Simons, Ric Spencer, and Ian O'Connell. He concluded that the show was "a highly enjoyable production, and it brought the fiftieth season of the Playmakers to a conclusion that sounded a note of much needed hope." The production of *Thirty-Seven Octobers*, directed by Patricia Barnett, was particularly enjoyed by Thomas Wolfe fans, who had the opportunity to see William Trotman and Malcolm Groome in two versions of the youthful Tom Wolfe-Eugene Gant.

The fiftieth anniversary is a good point from which to look back at the department's growth—or lack of growth—during the fifty years. During most of the Koch regime, the Dramatic Art courses were taught in the English Department. After the establishment of the Department of Dramatic Art in 1936, Dramatic Art majors were, of course, registered in that department. When Selden assumed the chairmanship in 1944, the University had an enrollment of 1,684 students and the Department of Dramatic Art had 35 students (25 undergraduates and 10 graduates). This represented a comparative low enrollment of the war years. By the academic year of 1946-47 there were 83 D.A. students (51 undergraduates and 32 graduates); but this number kept dropping during the 1950's until by the time Davis assumed the chairmanship in 1959 there were only 43 Dramatic Art majors (14 undergraduates and 29 graduates). This was approximately the same number of D.A. majors who were registered in 1944, but during these 15 years the University enrollment had increased from 1,684 to 7,959. Why was there not a similar increase in Dramatic Art?

Enrollment in Dramatic Art remained fairly constant in the early 1960's but showed a rather dramatic rise to 67 in 1963-64, with the establishment of the B.F.A. program. In 1964-65 there were 71 majors, in 1965-66 there were 80, and by 1967-68 the total had increased to 118 (30 A.B. candidates, 47 B.F.A., 40 M.A., and one Licentiate).

The academic year of 1968-69 showed a drop in enrollment from the high of 118 the year before to a total of 104 (64 undergraduates and 40 graduates). The draft probably accounted for part of this decrease but the low stipend offered to D.A. graduate student assistants was held responsible for the lack of increase in graduate students, who were receiving better aid offers elsewhere. The low stipend of $1,200 a year was increased to $2,400 for 1969-70. In spite of this increase, the 1969 fall registration showed only 19 graduate students and 57 undergraduates, a total of 76.

This lack of growth within the Department of Dramatic Art during the 1950's and early 1960's, when university enrollment at Chapel Hill and other institutions was increasing rapidly and when other departments of dramatic art were expanding, calls for some explanation. Student criticisms of the department for lack of excitement and unwillingness to experiment with lively contemporary drama undoubtedly provides one of the answers. The departmental staff, all old friends, old co-workers, all trained in the Koch tradition of the folk play and the use of native materials, were insulated—and isolated—from the fresh currents that were flowing in the American theatre in New York and in other theatre centers around the country. What was happening in New York did not seem to have much influence on what was happening in Chapel

Hill. Students—and prospective students—were probably more aware of this fact than were members of the staff.

At this point it is interesting to look back once more at the appraisal made by Norris Houghton in his book, *Advance from Broadway*, in 1941. After noting the criticisms made of The Playmakers by William Peery that the Carolina folk play "had been largely an escapist drama and had denied contemporary life," Houghton wrote: "The rich material for drama in Carolina or in New Hampshire, Arizona or Oregon is not only in the story that is ended. Folk dramatists live too much in the past; old tales spun out by the fire are more attractive to them than the news of the present. But yesterday is important to us only insofar as it illuminates our understanding and appreciation of today and fortifies our hope for tomorrow." The continued emphasis on the folk play and the constant absorption in the historical outdoor dramas had built a national reputation for The Carolina Playmakers, but both these obsessions had kept them from looking clearly at new movements in the theatre.

Plans for the 1969-70 Playmaker season indicated a new interest in contemporary drama with the selection of Harold Pinter's *The Caretaker* as one of the four major public productions, along with *Tartuffe, Dracula,* and *The Apple Tree.* Also planned were three studio productions in Graham Memorial, with public sale of tickets, and at least twelve workshop productions on Saturday mornings throughout the year to try out new plays and to give Dramatic Art students additional opportunities to act. Professor Russell Graves was named assistant department chairman and coordinator.

Mark Schoenberg directed his final play for The Playmakers in the summer of 1969, Tennessee Williams' *The Glass Menagerie,* before departing for a new job at the University of Alberta in Canada. His small cast of four, Jean Herring, Ric Spencer, Bill Donovan, and Kathryn Howell, received enthusiastic reviews. A bill of new one-act plays was also more favorably received than usual, especially a delightful children's fantasy, *The Accidental Ghost* by Linda Duck, and an amusing drama of college life and love and crossword puzzles, *Sixty-Nine Across* by Elizabeth

Russell Graves directing a scene from Pinter's *The Caretaker* (1969) with his three-man cast of Roger Howell, William Ellington, and Tim Toney.

Tanner, which included probably the boldest final curtain scene to have appeared on the Playmaker stage.

The summer of 1969 found The Carolina Playmakers looking back at the fifty-year celebration with mixed emotions and waiting to see what would happen next. Thomas Patterson, acting chairman of the Department of Dramatic Art, was still happily enjoying the novelty of having the use of Graham Memorial, secured primarily through his personal efforts, with enough room for offices, classrooms, rehearsal spaces, and even the costume shop. He was also hopeful of getting appropriations from the 1971 State Legislature for a new building since the University was placing the theatre building in a top priority of budget requests for the next biennium.

In the fall of 1969, John Whitty took over as Playmaker business manager and Clark Rogers as executive secretary of the Carolina Dramatic Association, both positions formerly held by John W. Parker. Mrs. Irene Smart Rains retired as costume director after a long and distinguished career as mistress of the costume room and confidante of the joys and woes of many a Playmaker. Three new members joined the staff: Mary Davis, costume director; Bruno Koch, assistant professor of acting; and Gordon Pearlman, technical director.

VII. After Fifty Years
--What Next?

One of Proff Koch's favorite remarks, after he had summarized the achievements of The Carolina Playmakers to some Chapel Hill audience of new students or some tour audience of strangers, was: "We've come a long way, haven't we, Sam?" And he would turn to Sam Selden for the always forthcoming corroboration. So now if The Playmakers stop at their fifty-year mark and try to look both ways, past and future, they, too, can say, with rightful pride: "We have come a long way." But if they are honest and if they are realistic, they would also have to say: "We've gone about as far as we can go—in the old direction." The one-act folk plays that made Koch and his early Playmakers famous across the nation are no longer understood, appreciated, or desired by the theatre public. They made their influence felt on the American drama and they brought fame to The Playmakers, but it is now necessary to look elsewhere for either a goal—or a gimmick.

The folk plays might be considered the "first phase" of Carolina Playmaker history. Then the enormously successful and influential outdoor dramas could be called a "second phase." At the fifty-year mark The Playmakers were looking for a third phase. What should it be?

In 1968-69 The Playmakers faced certain questions that revealed their dilemma—and their split personality. Is the objective of The Playmakers to train future playwrights, actors, directors, designers for the professional theatre, to turn out teachers of drama for colleges and high schools, or to produce appreciative theatre audiences of the future? Should The Playmakers select and produce plays that will provide the best training and experience for their drama students or provide satisfying entertainment for audiences that will pay their money to the box office? Can The Playmakers remain primarily a local or regional group concerned with dramatizing folklore, retelling history and presenting sociological, economic, racial, and psychological problems of the South or must they plunge into the mainstream of American life and the national theatre scene? Is there some new area in the American theatre where The Playmakers can focus their activity and their talents to give them a distinctive character of their own? With the day of the folk play swallowed up in the passage of time, how can they regain a distinctiveness that will differentiate them from any other competent university drama department?

The Playmaker staff may be wedded to the folk play and the outdoor drama through the rut of habit and the comfortable past. They may be suspicious of experimentation. They may be wary of stretching their talents and the capabilities of their students. But they are also creative men, thinking men, and men vitally concerned with the future of the theatre and a future for The Playmakers. They know a run-down alarm clock does not alarm. It does not strike the passing hours—or even know what time it is. So a committee was formed and has been working on plans for the future growing out of accomplishments of the past but not limited to traditions of the past. Tom Patterson, assistant chairman of the Department of Dramatic Art under Harry Davis, was chairman of the committee and serving with him were Russell Graves, Tommy Rezzuto, Mark Schoenberg, and Patricia Barnett. From their study have come recommendations that may provide a pattern for the future, a pattern that will also depend upon the individual who succeeds Davis as chairman and upon whether an adequate new theatre building will be provided by the University and the Legislature.

Facing the Problems

When Proff Koch taught one course in playwriting back in 1918 there was no great question about preparing students for their future careers. With the inauguration of the B.F.A. program, there is a definite and concerted effort being made to prepare students for professional careers, in acting, directing, or designing. The M.A. program is preparing students to teach drama in high schools or colleges; and if the projected Ph.D. program is established, it will train students for college or university teaching. A possible M.F.A. (Master of Fine Arts) program would be a terminal degree for the exceptionally gifted performing artist or technical student capable of intense practical work in his chosen field. And, of course, hundreds of Liberal Arts students take Dramatic Art courses as electives and gain a knowledge and understanding of the theatre that should make them more appreciative members of a theatre audience wherever they may be.

The art of the drama versus the lure of the box office presents a dilemma for any serious theatre group. Even the bustling, commercially minded dinner theatres know that *Any Wednesday* or *Under the Yum Yum Tree* draws in paying customers better than Shakespeare or Albee or Beckett. A Playmaker production of *My Fair Lady* or *Oklahoma* is more likely to be a sellout than *Long Day's Journey into Night* or *The Three Sisters*. When the Playmaker staff sits around the table and plans the next year's program, the voice of the box office has to be heard.

But what about the serious students (there are many these days) and the presumably intellectual faculty who cry for something "more imaginative," "more offbeat," "more experimental"? Behan's *The Hostage* drew more critical acclaim and enthusiasm from students in 1968 than the more popular or more standardized offerings.

Evidently there are two audiences—and The Playmakers need to appeal to both. One solution now being tried is to have two programs: a series of big popular productions for a wide public to be given in Memorial Hall or the Forest Theatre and another more specialized, more experimental series to be given in The Playmakers Theatre or in Graham Memorial for a smaller but discriminating audience. The 1968-69 season showed an attempt to try this solution by offering *Most Happy Fella, Becket, The Taming of the Shrew,* and the new Paul Green play for the larger audience while also offering a bill of one-acts, a new full-length original play, and a dramatic reading from Thomas Wolfe for the possibly smaller audience.

Parallel to the problem of play selection is the problem of casting. Should the plays be cast from drama students to give them theatre experience in acting a variety of roles, or should they be cast, with audience reception in mind, from the best available professional or semi-professional actors in the community or imported from New York?

Since its inception The Playmakers has been a community theatre, with all tryouts open to anyone around who wanted to try out. The early plays used the talents of Professors George McKie, Tigner Holmes, Richmond Bond, and many others. Through the years such professors as Earl Wynn, Walter Smith, Joel Carter, and William Hardy have taken leading roles, along with Dramatic Art Professors Harry Davis, Foster Fitz-Simons, Hubert Heffner, Kai Jurgensen, Lynn Gault, Tommy Rezzuto, Clark Rogers, Patricia Barnett, and John Whitty, Duke Professor Lloyd Borstelmann and local author Manly Wade Wellman. Faculty wives (Marion Fitz-Simons, Martha Nell Hardy, Jo Jurgensen, Cathy Orne) have appeared in numerous plays with real distinction; and so have such other actresses in the Chapel Hill community as Louise Lamont, Jo Pettis, and Marian Rosenzweig. Even Chapel Hill high school students have been in many plays (Patricia Simmons, Gloria di Costanza, Jock Lauterer, Mary Lindsay Spearman).

Such casting made exciting plays for the audience. But many a Dramatic Art major has complained ruefully: "There's no use for me to try out. Louise Lamont—or Marion Fitz-Simons or Kai Jurgensen—will get the part anyway." On the positive side is the fact that untried student actors can learn a great deal about the techniques of acting and about being at home on the stage by working in plays with more mature and experienced actors.

The very solution found in the problem of play selection may well work in this problem of casting. The major productions may still be thrown open to the best actor or actress available; but the "studio productions" or the smaller experimental productions may be confined to drama students, so they can get a better chance at leading roles and thus improve their own acting.

Repertory Theatre
Another possibility under consideration by The Playmakers in developing a program of two kinds of theatre is the establishment of a resident repertory company, with a nucleus of six to eight professional actors imported from New York or hired in the community to play the leading roles in major productions, supported by the more talented of the available student actors. Such a plan is in operation at Yale University, the Dallas Theatre Center (in co-operation with Trinity University in San Antonio), Stanford University, the McCarter Theatre at Princeton, and other institutions.

In his recent study of the contemporary theatre in the United States, *Beyond Broadway: The Quest for Permanent Theatres*, Julius Novick says: "Campus professional theatres make good sense: an academic community should provide an intelligent audience, and academic institutions are at least accustomed to deficit operations. . . . Some of the university companies are semi-autonomous bodies that exist only to put on plays for the academic community and the larger community that surrounds it; in other cases, the members of the company double as members of the faculty, and students participate alongside the professionals in the productions."

Certainly the area around Chapel Hill should be able to support a good repertory company, which could not only draw on the students and faculty of the University and nearby Duke University, but also on the rapidly growing population of the Research Triangle, which includes Chapel Hill, Durham, and Raleigh and the educational institutions in each city. In January, 1969, the North Carolina Arts Council granted The Playmakers $2,000 to investigate the feasibility of establishing such a resident company.

Outside Contacts
The Playmakers were born and raised in an insular environment,

with North Carolina playwrights writing plays from North Carolina materials to be acted by North Carolina casts for North Carolina audiences. Even when the playwrights came from Mexico and Canada and China and the audiences stretched along the Eastern seaboard, the emphasis was still on the folk play, whether one-act or full-length. The passing years have made this approach to the theatre both impractical and impossible, so the question for The Playmakers now is just how the approach should be widened and enlarged.

One of Samuel Selden's goals was to propel The Playmakers into the mainstream of American theatre. How effectively has this been done—and what techniques should be used today to hasten the plunge? Chapel Hill is only an hour and a half from New York by plane, but what concerted effort or planned program is made to encourage students to visit New York and see contemporary theatre on Broadway, off-Broadway, or off-off-Broadway?

In the summer of 1968, a staff member of the UNC English Department took 20 students to England by plane. In 21 days they saw 23 plays in London, Oxford, Stratford, and other places, talked to English actors, directors, designers, got a good view of the English theatre of today, wrote reviews and critiques of the plays they saw—and received three hours of college credit in English. Would not such a project be both possible and educational for the Dramatic Art Department? Certainly similar trips could be made to New York—or to Yale—or to the neighboring theatre productions of East Carolina University, The University of North Carolina at Greensboro, the Virginia Museum of Arts theatre, the School of the Arts in Winston-Salem, or the Frank Thompson Theatre or the Little Theatre in Raleigh. In the fall of 1969, Professor John Whitty made a beginning in this direction by taking a group of students to New York to see four plays in three days. If the only theatre work seen by UNC drama students is their own productions, they not only become more inbred and more insular, but have little concept of what is happening in the theatre world outside Chapel Hill.

Students read about exciting and ambitious new drama activity at Yale, but Robert Brustein had not visited Chapel Hill to talk about his innovations. Here again the fifty-year celebration was encouraging, for included on the year's program were talks by Tyrone Guthrie, Howard Taubman, and Robert Anderson. This should be an annual event—not just a fifty-year celebration.

What New Direction?

Perhaps the most salient question facing The Playmakers today is what new theatre area they might choose to explore in search of an approach that might be as pertinent, as lively, and as rewarding today as the native folk play was in 1918. What consciously chosen policy could be followed to make dramatic art at Chapel Hill distinct from dramatic art at any other institution?

One exciting idea that has come from the department itself through its Committee on Future Development is to emphasize American drama—not the limited field of the folk play, not the parochial encouragement of strictly North Carolina materials but an in-depth study of great American plays, an intensive development of new American playwrights, a focus on an aspect of the theatre that is not now being emphasized elsewhere.

This focus might begin with the establishment of a vigorous American-Playwrights-in-Residence program. The Writer-in-Residence Program at The University of North Carolina at Chapel Hill has been highly successful—from John Knowles and Reynolds Price to Norman Corwin, Carolyn Kizer, Max Steele, Herbert Gold, Robert Anderson, and Elizabeth Spencer.

The occasional production of a new play by an American playwright who just happened to be in Chapel Hill *(A Little to the Left* by Brock Brower, *The Marauders* by Noel Houston, *Darkening Shore* by Kermit Hunter, *Down to the Sea* by Kai Jurgensen, *The Battle of the Carnival and Lent* by Russell Graves, *The House of Connelly* by Paul Green, *Amen to a Mantis* by Randolph Umberger) is an indication of what The Playmakers could do for a playwright-in-residence by giving his latest play a good production so he can see what it looks like on the stage, giving students an opportunity to act in a new play, and inviting other theatre groups or New York producers to the premiere.

Chapel Hill would seem to be an ideal location for such an

American Play Center. Just as authors of early folk plays found North Carolina rich in folk material, picturesque speech, colorful characters, quaint superstitions, and usable historical incidents, so would present-day playwrights find in Chapel Hill excellent library facilities, strong resources in sociology, political science, and psychology departments, a lively concern for social problems, an expanding program in American Studies, an articulate and even critical student audience, and an additional potential audience drawn from the Research Triangle of Chapel Hill, Raleigh, and Durham.

The old "Chapel Hill Writers Group" of Paul Green, Betty Smith, James Street, Noel Houston, and John Ehle has been followed by a group of younger writers centered around Max Steele's creative writing program in the English Department, the Writer-in-Residence program, and the staffs of such magazines as *The Carolina Quarterly* and *Lillibulero*, and there is still a feeling of creative excitement in the literary air that would provide a congenial atmosphere for Playwrights-in-Residence. A really fresh and dynamic approach to establishing an American Play Center around The Carolina Playmakers and the Dramatic Art Department might also attract support and funds from various foundations interested in encouraging creative activities in the United States.

Obviously, the future of The Carolina Playmakers will depend, to a great extent, upon securing a new and adequate theatre in which to perform, the selection of a new department head with fresh ideas and the dynamism and energy with which to put them into effect, and a decision concerning the new direction The Playmakers will take, whether it be toward an American Play Center or some other distinctive approach.

But while resting upon this fifty-year plateau, The Playmakers might well ask themselves other questions about the present and the future. What is their attitude toward television, which is an area more likely to provide employment for Dramatic Art graduates than either the stage or the movies? The University of North Carolina has a unique opportunity to reach a wide viewing audience with its educational television outlet, with studios in Chapel Hill, Raleigh, and Greensboro, but very few locally originated programs are broadcast in spite of the wealth of talent available in both music and drama. National Educational Television programs are widely popular with viewers, many of whom find their most satisfying theatre experience watching NET plays.

Why should not this television experience include Playmaker plays? The audience is ready-made, the student actors need the television experience, and the material is certainly available. Of course, two University departments are concerned, the Department of Dramatic Art and the Department of Radio-Television-Motion Pictures, but a collaboration that could be so beneficial to both departments could surely be arranged. A new faculty member who might help bridge this gap is Paul Nickell, who holds his M.A. in Dramatic Art, is teaching in RTVMP, and has directed television plays in New York on "Omnibus," "Studio One," and "Playhouse 90," as well as numerous filmed television shows in Hollywood.

The National Educational Television network could already provide a natural outlet for some of the best Playmaker plays—and if the proposed public television network should become a reality, there should be an enormous demand for the kind of dramatic programs The Playmakers are capable of producing. Three short plays by Professor Russell Graves (*Being Wolfman, The Death and Marriage of Eva Braun in the Bunker,* and *A&P*) were broadcast by WUNC-TV in the fall of 1969.

Two other areas of Playmaker activity need rethinking today. The Junior Playmakers, which drew fifty enthusiastic high school students to Chapel Hill each summer for an intensive period of study and which fed a lively stream of talented young people into the University and into the Department of Dramatic Art, should by all means be re-established, with members of the staff given enough time and funds to provide an exciting program. A new appraisal should be made of the hundreds of original one-act plays that come out of the playwriting courses. In Koch's early days the best of these plays were not only produced in The Playmakers Theatre but also taken on tours and published in either the Carolina Play-book or in collected volumes. Now they simply disappear after one experimental production. Could the best of these plays be made available to high school and other college dramatic groups, either printed or mimeographed, either for a small royalty or free, for production in school assembly programs, Parent-Teacher meetings, or civic luncheon clubs?

University of North Carolina students have been frank in their appraisals of the current work of The Carolina Playmakers; and since these students both provide a large prospective audience and also represent a youthful point of view which may well give a clue to the tastes of future audiences, it might be enlightening to examine their criticisms.

During several recent semesters, students in a journalism book, play, and movie reviewing course were asked: "What suggestions would you make for improving the quality of Carolina Playmaker productions?" Almost invariably the replies came that acting was generally good, technical aspects of the productions (sets, costumes, lighting) were superior—but there are two basic weaknesses. One was the inadequacy of theatre facilities: The Playmakers Theatre too small, too crowded, too hot, too uncomfortable; Memorial Hall too large, too impersonal, too handicapped by poor acoustics. But the criticism that ran through all the replies and was often expressed quite sharply, was choice of plays. Here are some of the characteristic remarks:

"The sort of plays chosen is somewhat tame for an intellectual community. A little more spark and challenge in selection would help out—a few plays by Jean Genet, for example. The Playmakers do an adequate job. It's just that with more energy and daring they could really set people on fire around this campus."

"One thing seems perfectly clear. The sad fact is that The Playmakers have lately been given to a bad case of theatrical old age. There is great excitement in the theatre today. There is the new freedom of expression epitomized by *Hair*, the new sophistication about black and white in *The Great White Hope*, and the new feeling and spirit which has it that the audience ought not to be a passive receptacle for the spoken word. In short, things are happening in the theatre—but not really with The Carolina Playmakers. And this is a real shame for it seems clear to me that a college theatrical group, which is able to work from one night to the next without fear of financial disaster foreclosing the whole operation, is a likely place in which innovation and revolution in the theatre should occur. These are young people, after all, who are involved in these productions. They ought to have the opportunity to participate in the theatrical revolution which is in progress."

"The key problem this season seems to be the selection of plays. *Most Happy Fella* is a bore. The intensity and length of *Becket* was more than most audiences here could bear. The Playmakers do not have mass appeal on the campus due almost entirely to the fact that the group doesn't select many popular works. The Drama Department, at a crossroads now, must revitalize itself to keep up with other more exciting departments on other campuses. *The Hostage* is an example of how The Playmakers used their talents and produced a skillful and entertaining evening."

"The Playmakers should be more interested in new works, innovations in presentation, experimentation. For example, the Yale drama group received favorable attention recently for introducing the experimental new anti-war play, *We Bombed in New Haven*. We don't need a constant diet of Shakespeare, O'Neill, and Broadway musicals."

Perhaps the thread of criticism running through many of the student appraisals can be summed up in one thoughtful statement: "In a world where everything is being experimented with and where new ideas and inventions are being tried out every day, The Carolina Playmakers seem to be continually resurrecting antiques. The main improvement The Playmakers need is a change in attitude. Their spirit needs to be pepped up by a more adventurous and experimental outlook. Their resources are practically ready-made and their location on a progressive university campus are both good reasons why they should break out of their traditional bonds and present modern, if not experimental, theatre. The choice of plays is the first malady to be remedied. *Most Happy Fella* was an obscure, dated musical. As for *Becket*, everyone had seen the movie, which The Playmakers could not top. If they would choose plays relevant to the contemporary scene and innovate rather than renovate in their productions, the Playmaker appeal would be more broad and more worthwhile."

One after another of the student critics were critical of *Most Happy Fella, Ah, Wilderness!* and *The Trojan Women.* The one play that appeared to catch their interest and elicit their enthusiasm was *The Hostage.* Obviously, they felt that The Playmakers were still living too much in the dramatic past and were not sufficiently attuned to either the present or the future.

At this point it seems only fair to note that although the student critics were high in their praise of *The Hostage* and sharp in their criticism of *The Trojan Women* and *Ah, Wilderness!* the audience attendance during the 1967-68 season was highest (3,302) for *The Fantasticks* and lowest (2,167) for *The Trojan Women. The Hostage* came in the middle with an attendance of 2,260.

Year after year the largest audiences were brought out by popular Broadway musicals. Attendance in 1964-65 ranged from a low of 1,985 for Tennessee Williams' *A Streetcar Named Desire* to a high of 5,379 for *My Fair Lady.* In 1963-64, the audience ranged from a low of 1,526 for Eugene O'Neill's *Long Day's Journey into Night* to a high of 3,052 for Archibald MacLeish's *J. B.* And in 1962-63, the smallest attendance was 1,820 for *The Cherry Orchard* and the highest was 3,279 for *Guys and Dolls.* In 1962-63, the highly regarded production of Dylan Thomas' *Under Milk Wood* drew 1,631, a point somewhere between the low of 1,500 for *The Great Diamond Robbery* and the high of 3,951 for *South Pacific.* The conclusion seems to be that The Playmakers should reconsider their annual selection of plays to include at least one experimental or truly contemporary evening of drama to satisfy the "intellectual" segment of their audience, even though they still include popular musicals or Broadway hits to draw the larger box-office crowds.

While these criticisms of Playmaker plays were being voiced, other North Carolina theatre groups in Raleigh, Durham, and Greenville were producing Pinter's *The Homecoming* and *The*

Caretaker, Peter Weiss's *Marat/Sade*, Albee's *Who's Afraid of Virginia Woolf?* and Romulus Linney's new drama, *The Sorrows of Frederick*. The directors of these contemporary and "innovative" plays were frequently Playmaker alumni (Eugene Loessin and John Sneden at East Carolina University, Richard Parks at Duke University, Harry Callahan at the Raleigh Little Theatre) or even a Playmaker staff member (Mark Schoenberg at the Durham Allied Arts).

There is still, perhaps, not enough critical self-analysis. The very fact that members of the staff work well together and enjoy the warmth and camaraderie of a "Playmaker family," into which the Dramatic Art students are enthusiastically gathered, militates against a thoughtful and critical appraisal of each production, with constructive suggestions for improving the work of the department. If each staff member withholds his criticism of a production because the director is a confrere and old friend, then there is no basis for continued improvement of subsequent productions.

As The Carolina Playmakers enter their second half century, with a new department chairman to be selected and a new theatre building to be sought, present staff members still need to evaluate the work of The Carolina Playmakers and of the Department of Dramatic Art. The successful past can be nostalgically remembered with a soft look, but the future must be faced with a hard look. Whether the next chairman comes from within the department or from outside, a new direction must be marked out if the foundations set by Frederick Koch, Samuel Selden, and Harry Davis are to serve as a firm base for future building.

Index

This selective index lists only those Playmakers whose names appear two or more times in the text. These are merely representative of the thousands of actors, writers, and technicians who have worked in The Playmakers Theatre during these fifty years.